KB250868

반석

TOEFL
Final Test 3

급상승

반석

TOEFL 급상승 Final Test 3

저 자 박세연, 크리스틴 한, 빅토리아 신, 최종훈
발행인 고본화
발 행 반석출판사
2016년 2월 5일 초판 1쇄 인쇄
2016년 2월 10일 초판 1쇄 발행
홈페이지 www.bansok.co.kr
이메일 bansok@bansok.co.kr
블로그 blog.naver.com/bansokbooks

157-779 서울시 강서구 양천로 583번지 B동 904호
    (서울시 강서구 염창동 240-21번지 우림블루나인 비즈니스센터 B동 904호)
대표전화 02) 2093-3399 팩 스 02) 2093-3393
출 판 부 02) 2093-3395 영업부 02) 2093-3396
등록번호 제315-2008-000033호

Copyright ⓒ 박세연, 크리스틴 한, 빅토리아 신, 최종훈

ISBN 978-89-7172-776-8 (13740)

■ 교재 관련 문의: bansok@bansok.co.kr을 이용해 주시기 바랍니다.
■ 이 책에 게재된 내용의 일부 또는 전체를 무단으로 복제 및 발췌하는 것을 금합니다.
■ 파본 및 잘못된 제품은 구입처에서 교환해 드립니다.

반석

TOEFL
Final Test 3

영단기 최정예 강사진의 최단기 토플 실전 마무리 테스트

토 플 강의를 오랫동안 함께해 온 영단기 최정예 전문 강사들이 한데 모여 이 교재를 만들었습니다. 각 섹션별 전문가들의 노하우가 담긴 이 교재는 가장 최신의 출제경향에 맞춘 실전문제들과 앞으로 출제 가능성이 높은 문제들을 수록하고 있습니다.

그동안 저희 강사진은 토플 현장 강의 및 동영상강의를 통해 쌓은 많은 경험과 자료를 바탕으로 토플 교재의 새로운 패러다임을 만들기 위해 노력해왔습니다. 또한 토플을 준비하는 학생들의 입장에서 꼭 필요한 내용을 담기 위해 많은 시간을 투자했습니다.

이 교재는 토플 시험을 보기 전에 반드시 알아야 할 핵심적인 전략들을 제공하며, 본인의 실력을 객관적으로 평가해 볼 수 있도록 꾸몄습니다. 이 교재를 통해 여러분들은 실제 토플 테스트와 같은 경험을 해보고 자신의 장단점을 분석해 볼 수 있을 것입니다. 또한, 단순히 교재만 보는 것이 아니라, 이 교재의 내용을 다루는 동영상강의를 통해서 이해가 잘 안 되는 부분들도 완벽하게 집고 넘어갈 수 있습니다. (eng.dangi.co.kr)

저희 저자진은 앞으로도 많은 투자와 연구를 통해서 더 좋은 토플 교재를 만들도록 하겠습니다. 여러분의 유학 생활과 원대한 꿈을 이루는 데 도움이 되는 강사이자 친절한 도우미가 되도록 하겠습니다.

마지막으로, 이 교재를 출간하는 데 많은 도움을 주신 토플 연구진 및 반석출판사 대표님과 편집부원들에게 감사드립니다.

2016년 2월

Reading_ 박세연
Listening_ 크리스틴 한
Speaking_ 빅토리아 신
Writing_ 최종훈

목차

저자 약력

박세연 Reading 영단기 토플 오프라인 마감률 1위 강사

현) 영어단기학교 강남어학원 토플 리딩 대표강사
전) 파고다어학원 토플 리딩 강사(파고다어학원 Best Teacher상 수상)
    N파고다 토플 리딩 동영상 강의
- 뉴욕주립대 교육학 석사
- 저서 : iBT TOEFL Actual Test Reading – 파고다북스
        Voca For Toefl Reading – 파고다북스
- 동영상 강의 : 파고다 TOEFL VOCA for TOEFL Reading
        iBT TOEFL Reading 기본서

크리스틴 한 Listening 영단기 토플 인강매출 1위 강사

현) 영어단기학교 강남어학원 토플 리스닝 대표강사
    영어단기학교 토플 리스닝 동영상강의 대표강사
전) 해커스어학원 리스닝 강사
    파고다어학원 리스닝 강사
- Baruch College 회계학 석사
- The Pennsylvania State University 호텔경영 학사

빅토리아 신 Speaking 영단기 토플 오프라인 마감률 1위 강사

현) 영어단기학교 강남어학원 토플 스피킹 대표강사
    영어단기학교 토플 스피킹 동영상강의 대표강사
전) 파고다어학원(강남) 토플 스피킹 강사 만족도 1위
    N파고나 토플 스피킹 강사
- Case Western Reserve University 학사
- Darlington High School

최종훈 Writing 영단기 토플 오프라인 마감률 1위 강사

현) 영어단기학교 강남어학원 토플 라이팅 대표강사
    영어단기학교 토플 라이팅 동영상강의 대표강사
전) 파고다어학원 토플강사(파고다어학원 Best Teacher상 수상)
    National Service Center, Philadelphia, Pa ESL강사
- University of Pennsylvania Tesol 석사

최신의 토플 기출문제를 면밀하게 분석하여 실전문제와 유사한 난이도를 반영했다. 전체 문제에 대한 꼼꼼한 해석과 친절한 해설을 수록했기 때문에 혼자서 토플을 공부하는 수험생들에게 많은 도움이 될 것이다. 가장 최신의 토플 출제경향과 실전 난이도를 맞춘 이 교재는 토플 실전 마무리 테스트용으로 손색이 없다.

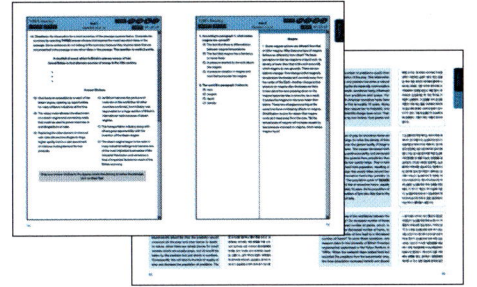

Reading_ 총 3세트 42문제를 제공한다.(1세트당 14문제) 세트당 시험 제한시간은 20분으로 설정하고 문제를 풀어보자.(총 60분)

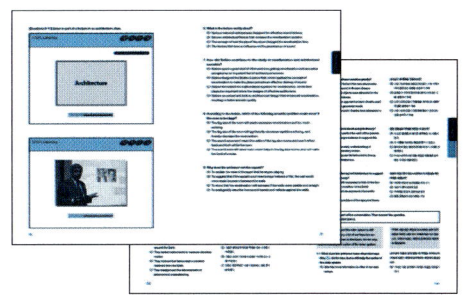

Listening_ 총 2세트 34문제를 제공한다.(세트당 대화문 1개 + 강의문 2개) 본 교재에서는 각 문제 사이의 간격을 30초로 설정했다.

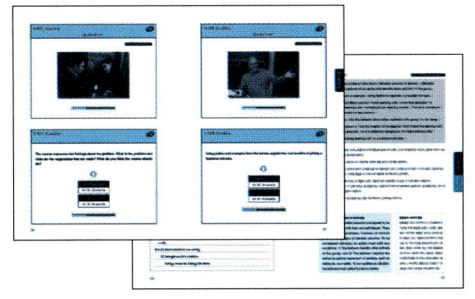

Speaking_ 제공된 음원을 들으면서 녹음기기를 이용하여 제한 시간 내에 답변을 한 후, 샘플 답안을 참고해보자.

Writing_ 각 태스크별로 제한된 시험 시간 안에 라이팅을 작성한 후, 해설의 샘플 답안을 참고하여 라이팅 기본기를 다져보자.

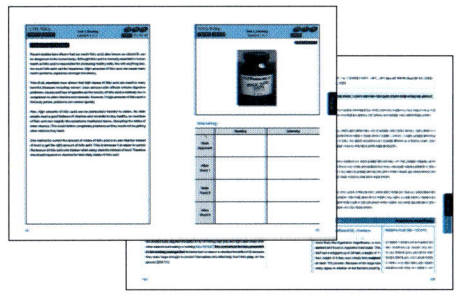

FINAL TEST 03

Reading

Reading Section Directions

This section measures your ability to understand academic passage in English.

Most questions are worth 1 point but the last question in each set is worth more than 1 point. The directions indicate how many points you may receive.

Some passages include a word of phrases that is underlined in blue. Click on the word of phrases to see a definition or an explanation.

Within each part, you can go to the next question by clicking **Next**. You may skip questions and go back to them later. If you want to return to previous questions, click on **Back**. You can click on **Review** at any time and the review screen will show you which questions you have answered and which you have not answered. From this review screen, you may go directly to any questions you have already seen in the Reading section.

During this test, you may click the **Pause** icon at any time. This will stop test until you decide to continue. You may continue the test in a few minutes or at any time during the period that your test is activated.

You may now begin the Reading section. In this part, you will read 1 passage. You will have 20 minutes to read the passage and answer the questions.

Click on **Continue** to go on.

TOEFL Reading

PAUSE TEST   SECTION EXIT

Part 1
Question 1 of 14

CONTINUE   REVIEW   HELP ?   BACK   NEXT

HIDE TIME   00 : 20 : 00

Reading

1. The word unprecedented in the passage is closest in meaning to
   Ⓐ prevailing
   Ⓑ fascinating
   Ⓒ novel
   Ⓓ thorough

2. According to paragraph 1, before the 1700's the source of energy for a majority of the machines was
   Ⓐ the waste produced by humans and animals
   Ⓑ huge technological leaps in wind and water energy
   Ⓒ mainly through non-mechanical sources
   Ⓓ using wood cut from adjacent areas as a source of fuel

3. The word available in the passage is closest in meaning to
   Ⓐ profuse
   Ⓑ valuable
   Ⓒ infinite
   Ⓓ reachable

4. According to paragraph 1, before the 1700's Britain's perilous energy situation was made because
   Ⓐ technology was not developed enough to use renewable energy sources
   Ⓑ overuse of traditional forms of energy was a culprit
   Ⓒ sufficient amount of trees were planted to burn for fuel
   Ⓓ there were no alternatives to support energy supply

The effect of steam engine

1 The unprecedented advancement of industry, technology, and economy known as the Industrial Revolution, and the factors of its realization, has been a source of debate among historians. Most technology before the 1700's was human or animal power-based but later developments harnessed the power of wind or water, which was highly beneficial for sailing and milling. Despite this technological growth, firewood was the main source of energy which was limited to its finite supply. Because of this factor, the Great Britain quickly ran out of available wood and faced an energy crisis. Coal, however, was available in large amounts under water, but there were no mechanized tools or machines that could be used to reach it. The steam engine would be the answer to this problem.

TOEFL Reading

PAUSE TEST   SECTION EXIT

Part 1
Question 5 of 14

CONTINUE   REVIEW   HELP ?   BACK ◀   NEXT ▶

HIDE TIME   00 : 20 : 00

5. Which of the following is true about steam engine in the paragraph 2?
   - Ⓐ It reduced the cost of the coal production.
   - Ⓑ It halted the exploitation of coal mines.
   - Ⓒ It solved the problem with the groundwater.
   - Ⓓ It could drill the ground, grind the soil and reach the deepest part in the ground.

6. The word contentedly in the passage is closest in meaning to
   - Ⓐ comprehensively
   - Ⓑ reasonably
   - Ⓒ satisfactorily
   - Ⓓ identically

7. What can be inferred about the building of mills after the introduction of the steam engine?
   - Ⓐ Steam engines made the cotton industry the most crucial industry in the Great Britain.
   - Ⓑ Bodies of water were no longer desired to power mills.
   - Ⓒ The placement of mill depended less on location than in the past.
   - Ⓓ Mills powered by steam engines had a larger output in creating goods than traditional mills due to more power.

8. In paragraph 2, why does the author mention the cotton industry?
   - Ⓐ To suggest the popularity of the engine in Britain
   - Ⓑ To show Britain's strength in the particular business
   - Ⓒ To show the effectiveness of the steam engines
   - Ⓓ To state the success of Britain's cotton industry to be responsible for half of all its exports

9. The word considerable in the passage is closest in meaning to
   - Ⓐ exceptional
   - Ⓑ exclusive
   - Ⓒ extrinsic
   - Ⓓ substantial

2 The first commercially available steam engine was invented and developed by James Watt at the turn of the 18th century which was affordable and effective. The mining industry was the first to espouse this new steam engine, using it to pump out groundwater from coal mines in order for miners to more contentedly reach the coal. The engines also allowed mills to function away from large moving bodies of water, which augmented the overall flexibility and efficiency in the location of mills. For example, a wheat mill could be built right next to a field of wheat. Furthermore, the addition of a rotary motor on the steam engines could connect the shafts used to drive machines. This increased the use of steam engines to various other industries including the cotton industry. Evidence for the effectiveness of the use of steam engines in the cotton industry can be seen in Britain's exponential growth of cotton output during this time. As a result, cloth made of cotton accounted for a considerable amount of Britain's international commerce. From the mid 1700's to the mid 1800's cotton exports multiplied by 230, a sixty fold increase in overall output. This totaled up to half of Britain's total exports.

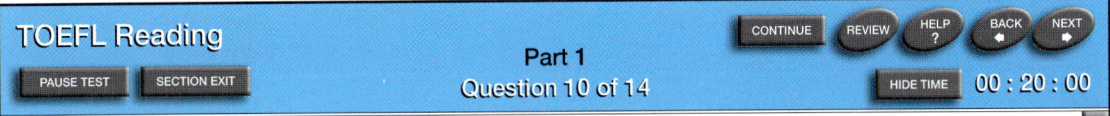
TOEFL Reading

PAUSE TEST   SECTION EXIT

CONTINUE   REVIEW   HELP ?   BACK   NEXT

Part 1
Question 10 of 14

HIDE TIME   00 : 20 : 00

Reading

3 Steam engines found many uses in a variety of industries. The introduction of steam engines improved productivity and technology, and allowed the creation of smaller and better engines. After the high-pressure engines were developed, transport-applications became possible, and steam engines found their way into railways, farms and road vehicles. Ⓐ ▪ Steam engines are examples of how changes brought by industrialization led to even more changes in other areas. The iron industry also was benefitted by the invention of the steam engine. Ⓑ ▪ Before the steam engine, charcoal, a form of burnt wood, was the main source of fuel for iron furnaces. However, as supply of charcoal could not meet the demand, coke as a replacement (because of the reduced cost) the iron industry helped to improve. Ⓒ ▪ Steam powered bellows with this material were quickly implemented within all corners of the iron industry, and output in iron radically increased. By 1850 the Great Britain produced more iron than the rest of the world combined. Ⓓ ▪

10. Look at the four squares [▪] that indicate where the following sentence could be added to the passage.

This is easily evident in the appreciable growth of the amount of iron produced by the country.

Where would the sentence best fit?

Click on a square [▪] to add the sentence to the passage.

11. Which of the sentences below best expresses the most important information in the highlighted section of the passage? *Incorrect answer choices change the meaning in important ways or leave out essential information.*

Ⓐ The Industrial Revolution would most likely have not been long and rooted in history if not for the steam engine's capacity to catalyze iron.

Ⓑ The platform of the entrenchment and length of the Industrial Revolution was the steam engine's role in further expanding the railroad industry.

Ⓒ The growth of the railroad industry through the combined technologies of the steam engine and iron resulted in an increase in the importance of the Industrial Revolution.

Ⓓ The synthesis of the steam engine and iron independently played the key role in expansion of the railroad industry through the entrenched prolongation of the Industrial Revolution.

12. According to the paragraph 4, what caused an increase in the demand for goods made by factories?

Ⓐ Products could be moved over long distances with lower shipping costs than ever before.

Ⓑ The steam powered locomotive could move trains without using horses.

Ⓒ Trains gained the ability to carry much larger loads than ever before.

Ⓓ Consumers were allowed to have fresher products made possible.

4 **The railroad industry was born from the developments of the steam engine and iron, further entrenching and lengthening the Industrial Revolution.** Up to this point, shipping heavy loads of freight across large distances was extremely expensive despite developments in canals and roads. Heavy loads carried out of mines were mostly done through the use of horsepower using parallel railroads. The steam locomotive usurped the transportation industry. Trains offered low-priced and fast procedures of transporting heavy loads of freight to reach far-away markets. The demand from the far away markets made the factories produce a myriad of products. Furthermore, profits made from the railroad industry were re-invested into other technologies and businesses. Low-skill laborers were needed to build these factories and tracks, year-round instead of seasonally. This resulted in an influx of people moving into larger cities to join this demographic increase.

TOEFL Reading

PAUSE TEST   SECTION EXIT

Part 1
Question 13 of 14

CONTINUE   REVIEW   HELP ?   BACK   NEXT

HIDE TIME   00 : 20 : 00

Reading

13. According to paragraph 4, which of the following did NOT happen after the invention of the steam locomotive?

Ⓐ Factories made a large amount of products in order to meet the steep increase of demand.

Ⓑ More railroads were built as fast as possible.

Ⓒ The working population increased in the cities.

Ⓓ Business opportunities opened up for railroad entrepreneurs in theirs and other industries.

4 The railroad industry was born from the developments of the steam engine and iron, further entrenching and lengthening the Industrial Revolution. Up to this point, shipping heavy loads of freight across large distances was extremely expensive despite developments in canals and roads. Heavy loads carried out of mines were mostly done through the use of horsepower using parallel railroads. The steam locomotive usurped the transportation industry. Trains offered low-priced and fast procedures of transporting heavy loads of freight to reach far-away markets. The demand from the far away markets made the factories produce a myriad of products. Furthermore, profits made from the railroad industry were re-invested into other technologies and businesses. Low-skill laborers were needed to build these factories and tracks, year-round instead of seasonally. This resulted in an influx of people moving into larger cities to join this demographic increase.

TOEFL Reading

PAUSE TEST   SECTION EXIT

Part 1
Question 14 of 14

CONTINUE   REVIEW   HELP ?   BACK   NEXT

HIDE TIME   00 : 20 : 00

14. Directions: An introduction for a short summary of the passage appears below. Complete the summary by selecting **THREE** answer choices that express the most important ideas in the passage. Some sentences do not belong in the summary because they express ideas that are not presented in the passage or are minor ideas in the passage. **This question is worth 2 points.**

A shortfall of wood, which is Britain's primary source of fuel,
forced Britain to find alternate sources of energy in the 18th century.

-
-
-

Answer Choices

Ⓐ Coal became accessible as a result of the steam engine, opening up opportunities for many different industries at the time.

Ⓑ The rotary motor allowed the attachment of a steam engine and connecting roads that could be used to power machines in a wide spectrum of uses.

Ⓒ Replacing the older element of charcoal with coke allowed iron forges to forge higher quality iron in a vast assortment of mixtures inciting demand for iron products.

Ⓓ As Britain became the producer of more iron in the world than all other countries combined, iron industry was responsible for a huge section of Britain's international trade because of steam engines.

Ⓔ The transportation industry along with others grew exponentially with the invention of the steam engine.

Ⓕ The steam engine began to be used in many industrial settings and became one of the most important businesses of the Industrial Revolution and served as a kind of important factors for much of the British economy.

Drag your answer choices to the spaces where they belong to review the passage,
click on **View Text.**

TOEFL Reading

PAUSE TEST   SECTION EXIT

Part 2
Question 1 of 14

CONTINUE   REVIEW   HELP ?   BACK   NEXT

HIDE TIME   00 : 20 : 00

1. According to paragraph 1, what makes magma rise upward?
    Ⓐ The fact that there is differentiation between magma temperatures
    Ⓑ The fact that magma has a tendency to move freely
    Ⓒ An increased pressure exerted by the rock above the magma
    Ⓓ A characteristic property variation in magma and rock that surrounds the magma

2. The word it in paragraph 1 refers to
    Ⓐ rock
    Ⓑ magma
    Ⓒ liquid
    Ⓓ density

Magma

1 Some magma actions are different from that of other magma. Why does one type of magma behave so differently from other? The basic perception is that as magma is a liquid rock, its density is lower than that of the rock around it, which magma to rise upwards. There are two distinct changes. One change is that magma's temperature decreases as it ascends away from the center of the Earth. Another change is that pressure on magma also decreases as there it rises since the rock pressing down on the magma becomes less in amounts; as a result, it causes the magma to rise even faster than before. These two changes occurring at the same time have contrasting effects on magma. Solidification occurs for reason that magma cools as it rises away from the core. Yet the temperature of magma will increase caused by less pressure imposed on magma, which keeps magma liquid.

TOEFL Reading

PAUSE TEST   SECTION EXIT

CONTINUE   REVIEW   HELP ?   BACK   NEXT

Part 2
Question 3 of 14

HIDE TIME   00 : 20 : 00

3. The word abundant in the passage is closest in meaning to
   Ⓐ profuse
   Ⓑ enormous
   Ⓒ crucial
   Ⓓ impending

4. Why does the author mention Hawaiian island according to the paragraph 2?
   Ⓐ To show it is the only example of mafic magma
   Ⓑ To show it demonstrates mafic magma contents
   Ⓒ To show the Hawaiian island has cool lava
   Ⓓ To show it is one of the common rocks in earth

5. According to paragraph 2, what can be inferred about silica content?
   Ⓐ The viscosity of the magma is chemical reaction of silica and the other elements.
   Ⓑ The speed of the magma is affected by the temperature of its silica and magnesium.
   Ⓒ Mafic magma is stiffer than felsic magma because of its movement.
   Ⓓ The amount of silica in magma determines the viscosity of magma.

2 The behaviors of magma can be comprehended by looking into their compositions. All magma contains gases and a mixture of simple elements. Magma can be divided into mafic magma, intermediate magma or felsic magma. Oxygen and silicon are the most abundant elements in magma, and geologists define magma types in terms of their silica content. These differences in chemical composition are directly related to differences in gas content, temperature, and viscosity. Mafic magma has relatively low silica content, roughly 50%, and higher contents in iron and magnesium. This type of magma has a low gas content and low viscosity, or resistance to flow. Mafic magma also has high mean temperatures, between 1000° and 2000°. Low viscosity means that mafic magma is the most fluid of magma types. It erupts non-explosively and moves very quickly when it reaches Earth's surface as lava. This lava cools into basalt, a rock that is heavy and dark in color due to its higher iron and magnesium levels. Basalt is one of the most common rocks in Earth's crust as well as the volcanic islands created by hot spots. The Hawaiian Islands are a direct result of mafic magma eruptions.

TOEFL Reading

CONTINUE   REVIEW   HELP ?   BACK   NEXT

PAUSE TEST   SECTION EXIT

Part 2
Question 6 of 14

HIDE TIME   00 : 20 : 00

Reading

6. The word <u>released</u> in the passage is closest in meaning to
Ⓐ infiltrated
Ⓑ discharged
Ⓒ percolated
Ⓓ recharged

7. Which of the sentences below best expresses the most important information in the highlighted section of the passage? *Incorrect answer choices change the meaning in important ways or leave out essential information.*
Ⓐ As intermediate magma releases lava, it increases the pressure below the earth's surface because of high thickness and gas content.
Ⓑ Under the earth surface, intermediate magma increases pressure high with high viscosity and high gas contents and, then it is discharged as lava.
Ⓒ Viscosity and gas content are the most crucial elements when intermediate magma builds up pressure.
Ⓓ Intermediate magma can be discharged as lava when magma has high viscosity and high gas content.

3 Intermediate magma has higher silica content than mafic magma. This results in a higher gas content and viscosity. Its mean temperature ranges from 800° to 1000° Celsius. As a result of its higher viscosity and gas content, intermediate magma builds up pressure below the Earth's surface before it can be released as lava. This more gaseous and sticky lava tends to explode violently and cools as andesite rock. Intermediate magma most commonly transforms into andesite due to the transfer of heat at convergent plate boundaries. Andesitic rocks are often found at continent of volcanic arcs, such as the Andes Mountains in South America, after which they are named.

TOEFL Reading

PAUSE TEST   SECTION EXIT

Part 2
Question 8 of 14

CONTINUE   REVIEW   HELP ?   BACK   NEXT

HIDE TIME   00 : 20 : 00

8. According to the paragraph 2, 3, which of the following are NOT components which cause magma to divide into three groups?

Ⓐ The behavior of magma is controlled by temperature.

Ⓑ Resistance to flow determines characteristics of magma.

Ⓒ The lava content determines how the magma behaves.

Ⓓ Silica contents in the rocks regulates the properties of magma.

9. According to paragraph 3, which of the following is true about andesitic rock?

Ⓐ It was the source of the Andes Mountains' name.

Ⓑ There is a tremendous pressure on the water from being squeezed into the andesitic rock.

Ⓒ The movement of the heat makes convert to andesitic rock from intermediate magma.

Ⓓ The downward force on the magma from the rock captures water contents within the andesitic rock.

3 Intermediate magma has higher silica content than mafic magma. This results in a higher gas content and viscosity. Its mean temperature ranges from 800° to 1000° Celsius. As a result of its higher viscosity and gas content, intermediate magma builds up pressure below the Earth's surface before it can be released as lava. This more gaseous and sticky lava tends to explode violently and cools as andesite rock. Intermediate magma most commonly transforms into andesite due to the transfer of heat at convergent plate boundaries. Andesitic rocks are often found at continent of volcanic arcs, such as the Andes Mountains in South America, after which they are named.

TOEFL Reading

PAUSE TEST   SECTION EXIT

CONTINUE   REVIEW   HELP ?   BACK   NEXT

Part 2
Question 10 of 14

HIDE TIME   00 : 20 : 00

10. What can be inferred about felsic magma's behavior in paragraph 4?

Ⓐ Felsic magma behaves more like a liquid than like a solid.

Ⓑ Felsic magma has 1% or 2% water that plays significant role.

Ⓒ Felsic magma is the magma seen in volcanic eruptions.

Ⓓ Felsic magma has a much lower point of solidification than mafic magma.

11. The word contemplate in passage is closest in meaning to

Ⓐ scrutinize

Ⓑ speculate

Ⓒ discourse

Ⓓ attribute

12. Which of the following is true about the pluton in paragraph 5?

Ⓐ Pluton is the hard crystalized plate above the earth's crust.

Ⓑ Pluton is formed when magma cools slowly.

Ⓒ Pluton is the most critical component because of the elasticity.

Ⓓ Pluton is a melted volcano which is several kilometers in height.

4 Felsic magma has the highest silica content of all magma types, between 65-70%. As a result, felsic magma also has the highest gas content and viscosity, and lowest mean temperatures, between 650° and 800° Celsius. Thick, viscous felsic magma can trap gas bubbles in a volcano's magma chamber. These trapped bubbles can cause explosive and destructive eruptions. These eruptions eject lava violently into the air, which cools into igneous, volcanic rock. Much like intermediate magma, felsic magma may be most commonly found at convergent plate boundaries where transfer of heat and flux melting create large stratovolcanoes.

5 Another point to contemplate is what happens after the solidification takes place. Crystallized form is made from magma slowly cooling below the surface of the earth. Ⓐ ▪ Plutons are much higher in density compared to that of the earth's crust. In practice, pluton usually refers to a distinctive mass of igneous rock, typically several kilometers in dimension. Ⓑ ▪ Plutons can push through the crust due to the elasticity. Ⓒ ▪ The foundation of the earth's crust is very boiling and it gets softer as the temperature rises and become rigid as it cools. So, the Plutons will push upwards underneath the crust where the rock is hot. Ⓓ ▪

TOEFL Reading

PAUSE TEST   SECTION EXIT

Part 2
Question 13 of 14

CONTINUE   REVIEW   HELP ?   BACK   NEXT

HIDE TIME   00 : 20 : 00

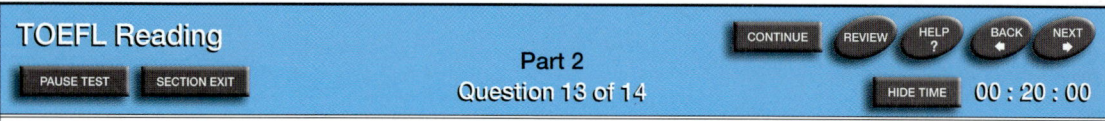

5   Another point to contemplate is what happens after the solidification takes place. Crystallized form is made from magma slowly cooling below the surface of the earth. Ⓐ ▪ Plutons are much higher in density compared to that of the earth's crust. In practice, pluton usually refers to a distinctive mass of igneous rock, typically several kilometers in dimension. Ⓑ ▪ Plutons can push through the crust due to the elasticity. Ⓒ ▪ The foundation of the earth's crust is very boiling and it gets softer as the temperature rises and become rigid as it cools. So, the Plutons will push upwards underneath the crust where the rock is hot. Ⓓ ▪

13. Look at the four squares [▪] that indicate where the following sentence could be added to the passage.

The solidified magma formed below the earth's crust is called Plutons.

Where would the sentence best fit?

Click on a square [▪] to add the sentence to the passage.

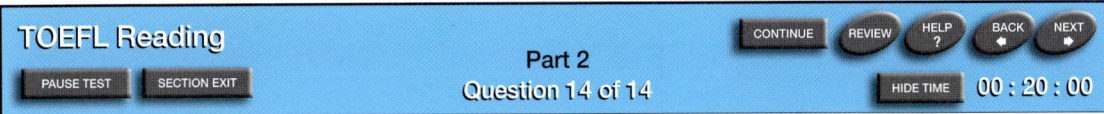

TOEFL Reading

PAUSE TEST   SECTION EXIT

CONTINUE   REVIEW   HELP ?   BACK   NEXT

Part 2
Question 14 of 14

HIDE TIME   00 : 20 : 00

Reading

14. Directions: An introduction for a short summary of the passage appears below. Complete the summary by selecting the **THREE** answer choices that mention the most important points in the passage. Some sentences do not belong in the summary.

> Magma is a mixture of molten rocks that is found beneath the surface of the Earth and is divided into different kinds.

- •
- •
- •

Answer Choices

Ⓐ The specific proportions of minerals in the magma determine how the magma behaves.

Ⓑ Mafic magma contains 50% silica content and its mean temperature is between 1000° and 2000° while Intermediate magma's mean temperature ranges from 800° to 1000°C.

Ⓒ Silicate in the magma determines the viscosity of the magma, which has a direct effect on how ease the magma move.

Ⓓ Differences in chemical composition are directly related to differences in gas content, temperature, and viscosity.

Ⓔ Mafic magma has more violent eruptions than felsic volcanoes since their properties enable them to act much like fluid.

Ⓕ Mafic volcanoes are the most common and the Hawaiian Islands are the best example of places made by mafic magma.

Drag your answer choices to the spaces where they belong to review the passage, click on **View Text**.

TOEFL Reading

PAUSE TEST   SECTION EXIT

Part 3
Question 1 of 14

CONTINUE   REVIEW   HELP ?   BACK   NEXT

HIDE TIME   00 : 20 : 00

1. The word adequate in the passage is closest in meaning to
   - Ⓐ innovative
   - Ⓑ certain
   - Ⓒ crucial
   - Ⓓ sufficient

2. According to paragraph 1, which of the following is NOT the role of water in plant life that lives in desert environments?
   - Ⓐ It is crucial for photosynthetic processes.
   - Ⓑ If a certain amount of water is not satisfied, the plant will die.
   - Ⓒ Transporting nutrients is one of the roles in water.
   - Ⓓ Soil texture is determined by plant's physical ability.

Plants and animals in Deserts

1 The ability to deal with extreme heat is indispensable for plants and animals that occupy the desert. Water is an essential element in plant and animal survival in the desert due to the aridity of the habitat. All organisms require an adequate amount of water to survive. If the threshold is breached, organisms will die. Water is critical in ferrying nutrients throughout the plant and in serving as the foremost raw material in the photosynthetic process. A plant's ability to expand its body structure depends on the availability of water, soil texture, topographical distributions, and the proximity of large bodies of water. These elements account for why some areas cannot support any plant life and others have dense areas of plant growth. For this reason, rainforests have up to 100 times more plant life than in deserts in the same amount of land.

TOEFL Reading

PAUSE TEST   SECTION EXIT

CONTINUE   REVIEW   HELP?   BACK   NEXT

Part 3
Question 3 of 14

HIDE TIME   00 : 20 : 00

3. What can be inferred about ephemerals in paragraph 2?
   - ⒜ They need water to survive in the desert.
   - ⒝ They photosynthesize at a fast rate at any location.
   - ⒞ They need more water to survive in environment than do perennials.
   - ⒟ They take a long time to grow.

4. In what way is paragraph 2 presented?
   - ⒜ Types of plants are identified and the weaker type is focused on.
   - ⒝ The author lists the names of plants.
   - ⒞ The author splits the plants into two groups and lists the flaws of each group.
   - ⒟ The author categorizes the plants into two groups and explains the characteristic of the plants.

5. The word withstand in the passage is closest in meaning to
   - ⒜ endure
   - ⒝ assemble
   - ⒞ follow
   - ⒟ resemble

6. Which of the following is NOT mentioned about perennial adaptation?
   - ⒜ They have dense hair to cover leaves on their plants.
   - ⒝ They control their body size.
   - ⒞ They have extensive root system.
   - ⒟ They hide in their environments.

7. Why does the author mention cacti in paragraph 2?
   - ⒜ To indicate that the plant can be seen in the extremely hot area
   - ⒝ To provide an example of plants that shows how plants deal with the deficiency of water when water is desperate
   - ⒞ To represent that cacti develop external coating to prevent water ventilation
   - ⒟ To give an example of the plant having extension of roots

2 Most plants of the desert fall into two main categories. The first is short-living ephemerals. The second is long-living perennials. The entire desert plants are under the above mentioned categories. When a certain level of rainfall is available, ephemerals absorb the water rapidly and grow vigorously, producing large quantities of fruits and flowers due to their short life cycles. However, immediate death ensues when there is not an adequate amount of water to sustain its growth as plants do not have any organic mechanisms to retain fluids. Fortunately, these plants successfully finish their cycle and plant their seeds before this occurs. These seeds lay dormant under the soil throughout the period of drought, and grow once the weather is favorable and wet. The long-living perennials have developed several different survival mechanisms to withstand dry seasons. Most of these perennials grow extremely dense hairs to cover waxy leaves to prevent water loss through evaporation while others limit their growth to low heights and wide widths to lay down extensive root systems. That people can see many of these plants which have root systems that easily stretch beyond ten meters underground in all directions is not unfamiliar. Succulents are able to keep water within their systems in times of desperate need as seen in cacti. Other plants have evolved a type of hard woody shell to prevent an external collapse due to the lack of water in its interior. Phreatophytes are another type of perennial that grows extremely long roots in search of a guaranteed pool of underground water. Some examples include date trees and tamarinds.

TOEFL Reading

PAUSE TEST   SECTION EXIT

Part 3
Question 8 of 14

CONTINUE   REVIEW   HELP ?   BACK   NEXT

HIDE TIME   00 : 20 : 00

8. The word stationary in the passage is closest in meaning to
   Ⓐ wandering
   Ⓑ immobile
   Ⓒ primitive
   Ⓓ secured

9. According to paragraph 3, which of the following best explains the term aestivation?
   Ⓐ It is a decrease in physiological processes in an area away from the heat.
   Ⓑ It is the more favorable adaptation than other tactics.
   Ⓒ An animal is no longer able to facilitate normal functioning.
   Ⓓ An animal becomes dormant for a certain period every year.

10. Which of the sentences below best expresses the most important information in the highlighted section of the passage? *Incorrect answer choices change the meaning in important ways or leave out essential information.*
    Ⓐ A shaded cave provides animals with high level of adaptability of dormancy.
    Ⓑ Dormancy is an adaptation which enables animals to adapt to their pleasant habitats such as in a shaded cave.
    Ⓒ Aestivation helps animals escape from heat with minimized metabolic rates in hospitable setting.
    Ⓓ Whether animals can endure certain amount of heat or not has little to do with their survival in the friendly environment.

3 Animals are not so stationary like plants that they have developed behavioral instincts to survive in extreme temperature of the deserts. Most animals either retreat or escape the heat. Aestivation is one method of escaping the heat by going under a state of torpidity or dormancy in a friendly environment such as in a shaded cave. This survival tactic is mostly seen in reptiles and amphibians of the desert as the animal is able to almost stop all of its bodily processes and decrease overall temperature. Dormancy of this manner requires fewer nutrients to survive and is required in overcoming droughts. It is not until favorable conditions that the animals can return to a normal state. However, it is a quite 'light' state of dormancy. A study done on snails which are native to parts of Europe and Northern Africa shows that they can wake from their dormant state within ten minutes of being introduced to a wetter environment. The migration of animals in different seasons is another method of defeating the desert heat. Birds and mammals are mainly responsible for this survival tactic. Some animals cannot endure the extreme heat, and they escape by migrating a handful of miles out of a valley and up into the mountains. Mule deer in the American southwest seasonally complete this cycle between mountain and desert, as do juncoes, white-crowned sparrows and goshawks. Ⓐ ▪ The daily living cycle of animals involves retreat as it is only a temporary escape from the dry and heat. Ⓑ ▪ For example, during the hottest hours of a particular day, birds will rest under the refuge of a shaded nest. Ⓒ ▪ Mammals also use a similar method as seen in kangaroo rat that will dig its way underground during these times. Ⓓ ▪

TOEFL Reading

PAUSE TEST   SECTION EXIT

CONTINUE   REVIEW   HELP ?   BACK   NEXT

Part 3
Question 11 of 14

HIDE TIME   00 : 20 : 00

Reading

11. The word they in the passage refers to
Ⓐ birds
Ⓑ mammals
Ⓒ snails
Ⓓ animals

12. According to the paragraph 4, which animal has different type of adaptation from others?
Ⓐ Mule deer
Ⓑ Mammals
Ⓒ Sparrows
Ⓓ Snails

3 Animals are not so stationary like plants that they have developed behavioral instincts to survive in extreme temperature of the deserts. Most animals either retreat or escape the heat. Aestivation is one method of escaping the heat by going under a state of torpidity or dormancy in a friendly environment such as in a shaded cave. This survival tactic is mostly seen in reptiles and amphibians of the desert as the animal is able to almost stop all of its bodily processes and decrease overall temperature. Dormancy of this manner requires fewer nutrients to survive and is required in overcoming droughts. It is not until favorable conditions that the animals can return to a normal state. However, it is a quite 'light' state of dormancy. A study done on snails which are native to parts of Europe and Northern Africa shows that they can wake from their dormant state within ten minutes of being introduced to a wetter environment. The migration of animals in different seasons is another method of defeating the desert heat. Birds and mammals are mainly responsible for this survival tactic. Some animals cannot endure the extreme heat, and they escape by migrating a handful of miles out of a valley and up into the mountains. Mule deer in the American southwest seasonally complete this cycle between mountain and desert, as do juncoes, white-crowned sparrows and goshawks. Ⓐ ■ The daily living cycle of animals involves retreat as it is only a temporary escape from the dry and heat. Ⓑ ■ For example, during the hottest hours of a particular day, birds will rest under the refuge of a shaded nest. Ⓒ ■ Mammals also use a similar method as seen in kangaroo rat that will dig its way underground during these times. Ⓓ ■

TOEFL Reading

CONTINUE   REVIEW   HELP ?   BACK   NEXT

PAUSE TEST   SECTION EXIT

Part 3
Question 13 of 14

HIDE TIME   00 : 20 : 00

3 Animals are not so stationary like plants that they have developed behavioral instincts to survive in extreme temperature of the deserts. Most animals either retreat or escape the heat. Aestivation is one method of escaping the heat by going under a state of torpidity or dormancy in a friendly environment such as in a shaded cave. This survival tactic is mostly seen in reptiles and amphibians of the desert as the animal is able to almost stop all of its bodily processes and decrease overall temperature. Dormancy of this manner requires fewer nutrients to survive and is required in overcoming droughts. It is not until favorable conditions that the animals can return to a normal state. However, it is a quite 'light' state of dormancy. A study done on snails which are native to parts of Europe and Northern Africa shows that they can wake from their dormant state within ten minutes of being introduced to a wetter environment. The migration of animals in different seasons is another method of defeating the desert heat. Birds and mammals are mainly responsible for this survival tactic. Some animals cannot endure the extreme heat, and they escape by migrating a handful of miles out of a valley and up into the mountains. Mule deer in the American southwest seasonally complete this cycle between mountain and desert, as do juncoes, white-crowned sparrows and goshawks. Ⓐ ■ The daily living cycle of animals involves retreat as it is only a temporary escape from the dry and heat. Ⓑ ■ For example, during the hottest hours of a particular day, birds will rest under the refuge of a shaded nest. Ⓒ ■ Mammals also use a similar method as seen in kangaroo rat that will dig its way underground during these times. Ⓓ ■

13. Look at the four squares [■] that indicate where the following sentence could be added to the passage.

Advantages of such burrows include the coolness of the earth.

Where would the sentence best fit?

Click on a square [■] to add the sentence to the passage.

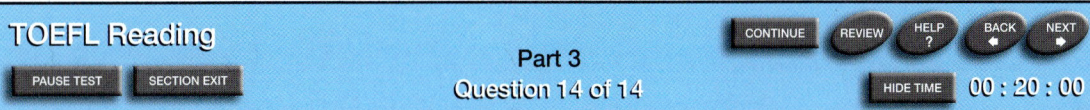

TOEFL Reading

PAUSE TEST   SECTION EXIT

CONTINUE   REVIEW   HELP ?   BACK   NEXT

Part 3
Question 14 of 14

HIDE TIME   00 : 20 : 00

Reading

14. Directions: An introduction for a short summary of the passage appears below. Complete the summary by selecting the **THREE** answer choices that mention the most important points in the passage. Some sentences do not belong in the summary.

In plants that are found in desert environments, water is essential in a variety of different aspects that affect the amount of its growth and area of its distribution.

-
-
-

Answer Choices

Ⓐ There are two families of desert plants and each group has disparate survival skills made toward living in drought situations.

Ⓑ Ephemerals quickly grow and die just as fast, planting seeds that do not emerge until a certain amount of water becomes available in the wet season.

Ⓒ Some of the evolutionary adaptations for plants that are able to live during the dry season involve finishing their reproductive cycle promptly and coatings on the plant, the ability to store water, and extremely large root structures that continuously search for water.

Ⓓ Animals can either escape the heat through aestivation, or migration and retreat by staying in cool places during the hottest part of the day.

Ⓔ While mammals choose to dig into the ground to retreat from the heat, reptiles and amphibians are physically adapted to deserts as they are able to go into a state of dormancy.

Ⓕ Behavioral or physical adaptions are present in all animals in order for them to find survival success in deserts.

Drag your answer choices to the spaces where they belong to review the passage, click on **View Text**.

반석
TOEFL 립성
Final Test 3

Listening

Listening Section Directions

This section measures your ability to understand conversations and lectures in English. The listening section is divided into 2 separately timed parts. In each part you will listen to 1 conversation and 2 lectures. You will hear each conversation or lecture only one time.

After each conversation or lecture, you will answer some questions about it. The questions typically ask about the main idea and supporting details. Some questions ask about a speaker s purpose and attitude. Answer the questions based on what is stated or implied by the speakers.

You may take notes while you listen. You may use your notes to help you answer the questions. Your notes will not be scored.

If you need to change the volume while you listen, click on the Volume icon at the top of the screen.

In some questions, you will see this icon: ∩ This means that you will hear, but not see part of the question. Some of the questions have special directions. These directions appear in a gray box on the screen.

Most questions are worth one point. If a question is worth more than one point, it will have special directions that indicate how many points you can receive.

You must answer each question. After you answer, click on Next. Then click on OK to confirm your answer and go on to the next question. After you click on OK, you cannot return to previous questions.

Test3_Listening_Part1_00_Direction.mp3

Listening Directions

In this part, you will listen to 1 conversation and 2 lectures.

You must answer each question. After you answer, click on Next. Then click on OK to confirm your answer and go on to the next question. After you click on OK, you cannot return to previous questions.

You may now begin this part of the Listening Section.

Listening

[Questions 1-5] Listen to part of a conversation between a student and staff member.

TOEFL Listening

VOLUME ◀   HELP ?   OK   NEXT ▶

Test3_Listening_Part1_01-05.mp3

1. What is the conversation mainly about?
   Ⓐ Inviting public speakers for a club event
   Ⓑ Signing up for an established club
   Ⓒ Managing a school activity
   Ⓓ Completing registration for a school club

2. Why does the woman offer a semi-private office?
   Ⓐ Because only registered clubs can get private offices
   Ⓑ Because space is limited on campus
   Ⓒ Because the photography club has any few members
   Ⓓ Because the student cannot afford a private office

3. Why does the woman ask the name of the faculty advisor?
   Ⓐ Because she is planning to question the faculty advisor about the club
   Ⓑ Because she is trying to check the status of the club on her computer
   Ⓒ Because she is confirming that the club has an official supervisor
   Ⓓ Because she has no idea how to help the student

Listen again to a part of the conversation. Then answer the question.

4. Why does the woman say this: 🎧
    Ⓐ To attempt to help the student in a polite fashion
    Ⓑ To express doubt about the establishment of the club
    Ⓒ To suggest that there are too many photography clubs
    Ⓓ To make conversation while searching for the records

5. What will the student probably do following the conversation?
    Ⓐ Return to his dormitory room
    Ⓑ Register his club officially
    Ⓒ Check the office he has been given
    Ⓓ Gather members for his club

[Questions 6-11] Listen to part of a lecture in an architecture class.

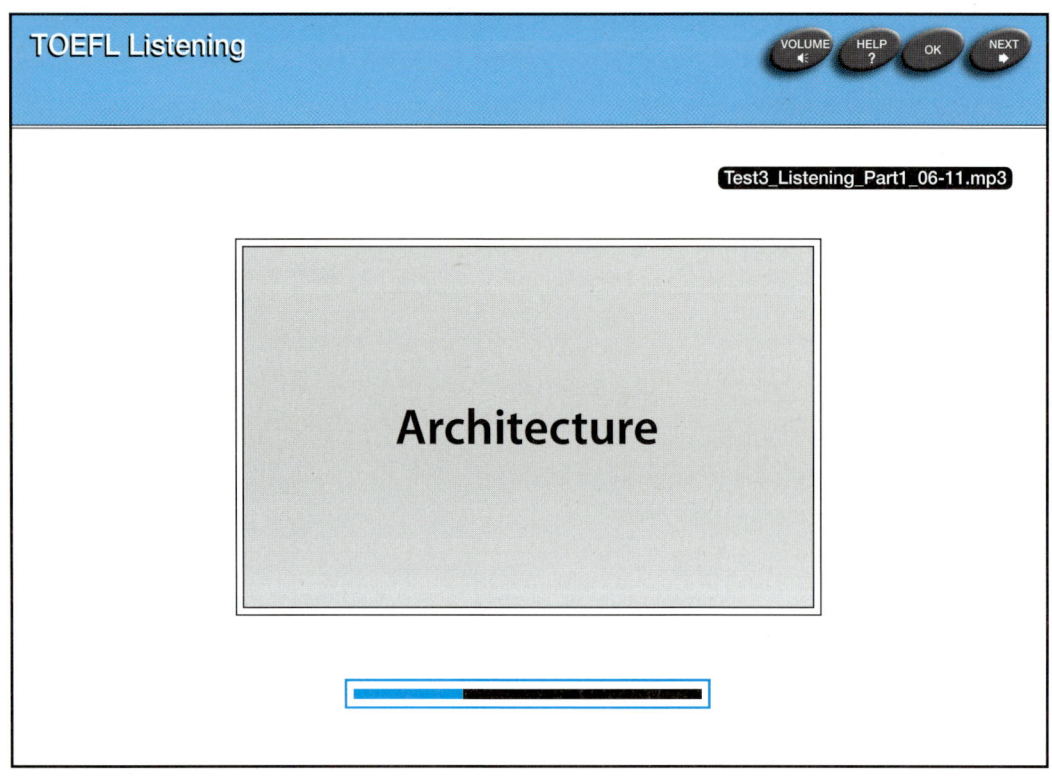

6. What is the lecture mainly about?
   Ⓐ Various historical architectures designed for effective sound delivery
   Ⓑ Various architectural factors that increase the reverberation duration
   Ⓒ The concept of how the size of the room changes the reverberation time
   Ⓓ The factors that have an influence on the persistence of sound

7. How did Sabine contribute to the study of reverberation and architectural acoustics?
   Ⓐ Sabine spent a great deal of effort and time getting reverberation and acoustics accepted as an important fied of architectural science.
   Ⓑ Sabine designed the Boston Lecture Hall, which applied his concept of reverberation to make the place promote an effective delivery of sound.
   Ⓒ Sabine formulated the mathematical equation for reverberation, which later played an important role in the designs of effective auditoriums.
   Ⓓ Sabine conceived and built an architectural design that enhanced reverberation, resulting in better acoustic quality.

8. According to the lecture, which of the following acoustic problem could occur if the room is too large?
   Ⓐ The big size of the room will create excessive reverberation and too much echoing.
   Ⓑ The big size of the room will significantly decrease repetitive echoing, and thereby decrease the reverberation.
   Ⓒ The sound wave won't reach the walls of the big size rooms and won't reflect back and forth within the room.
   Ⓓ The sound wave will travel much more freely in the big size rooms, and will make too loud of a noise.

9. Why does the professor mention squash?
   Ⓐ To explain the rules of the sport that he enjoys playing
   Ⓑ To suggest that if the squash court was bumpy instead of flat, the ball would more easily bounce in between the walls
   Ⓒ To show that the reverberation will increase if the walls were parallel and straight
   Ⓓ To analogically describe how sound travels and reflects against the walls

10. According to the lecture, which of the following architectural properties will promote or demote reverberation? If a property is not mentioned in the lecture or does not apply to either of choices, click on neither.

	Promote	Demote	Neither
Largely spaced rooms			
Oval shaped architectures			
Flat and parallel walls			
Ceiling chandeliers			

Listen again to a part of the conversation. Then answer the question.

---

11. What can be inferred when the professor says this: 🎧
    Ⓐ It is hard to plan an architectural design that satisfies people of various artistic preferences.
    Ⓑ The quality of sound can have a great influence on a wide range of situations.
    Ⓒ It is a difficult task to create architecture that is expected to last for long periods of time.
    Ⓓ There are many speakers and musicians who are picky about architectural acoustics.

[Questions 12-17] Listen to part of a lecture in a psychology class.

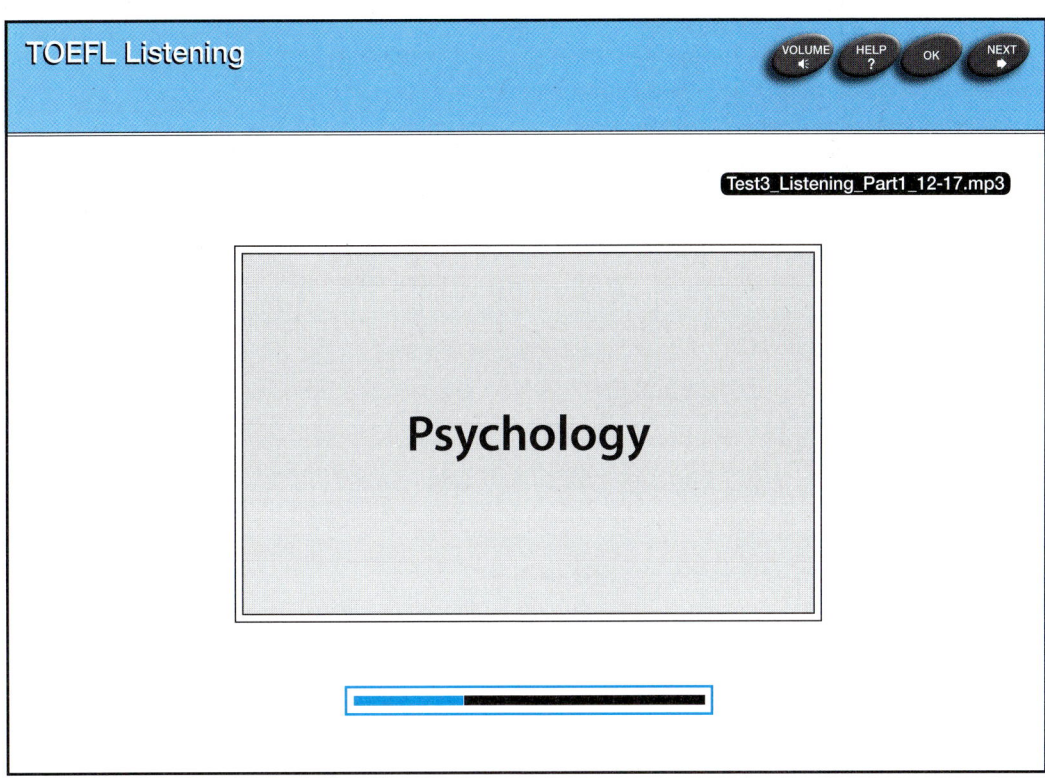

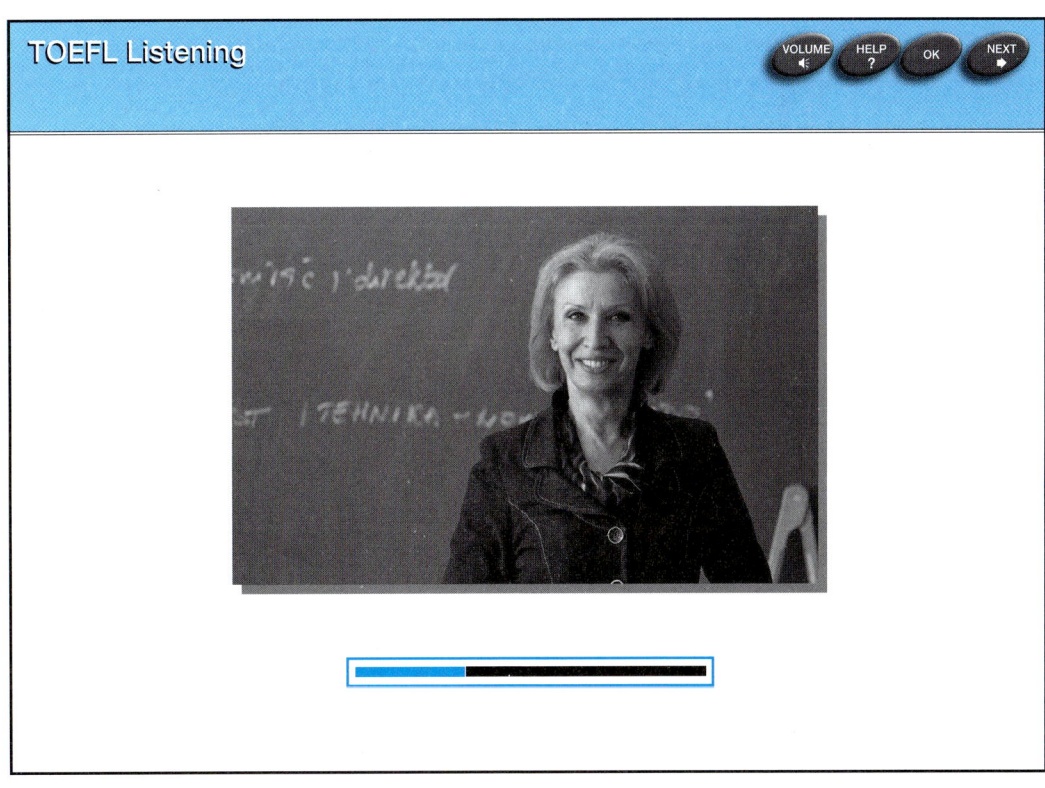

12. What does the professor primarily discuss?
    Ⓐ The reason why researchers are interested in animal psychology
    Ⓑ The extent of research on the intelligence of dolphins and monkeys
    Ⓒ The disadvantages of food rewards in studies involving animals
    Ⓓ The studies concerning animals' awareness of feeling uncertainty

13. Why do researchers study animal cognition?
    Ⓐ To analyze the feelings and mental states that animals can experience
    Ⓑ To prove that some species of animals exhibit high levels of intelligence
    Ⓒ To understand mental capabilities of animals compared to those of humans
    Ⓓ To investigate the thought pattern behind animals and humans make

14. According to the professor, why are dolphins and monkeys utilized for psychological research?
    Ⓐ They perform well on intelligence tests.
    Ⓑ They have developed brains similar to those of humans.
    Ⓒ They can be disciplined to carry out specific actions.
    Ⓓ They understand human speech and communication.

15. What was the purpose of the pass paddle in the dolphin study?
    Ⓐ It was the correct option for blocks that were neither round nor square.
    Ⓑ It increased the probability that the dolphins would make the right choice.
    Ⓒ It showed the difficulty of the experiment.
    Ⓓ It attempted to demonstrate that dolphins could feel unsure.

16. Why did some researchers disagree with the conclusion of the dolphin study?
    Ⓐ Mental capacities of dolphins cannot be compared to those of humans
    Ⓑ Responses could result from learned association rather than cognition.
    Ⓒ Options were unnecessarily numerous and confusing for the dolphins.
    Ⓓ Dolphins only chose the third option to avoid punishment.

17. Why did each experiment in the monkey study consist of four trials?
    Ⓐ To increase the accuracy of the experiment by conducting multiple trials
    Ⓑ To lengthen the time required for the completion of the experiment
    Ⓒ To prevent the monkeys from taking advantage of the pass option
    Ⓓ To raise the difficulty of the experiment by showing several colors

Test3_Listening_Part2_00_Direction.mp3

Listening Directions

In this part, you will listen to 1 conversation and 2 lectures.

You must answer each question. After you answer, click on Next. Then click on OK to confirm your answer and go on to the next question. After you click on OK, you cannot return to previous questions.

You may now begin this part of the Listening Section.

Listening

[Questions 1-5] Listen to part of a conversation between a student and a clerk.

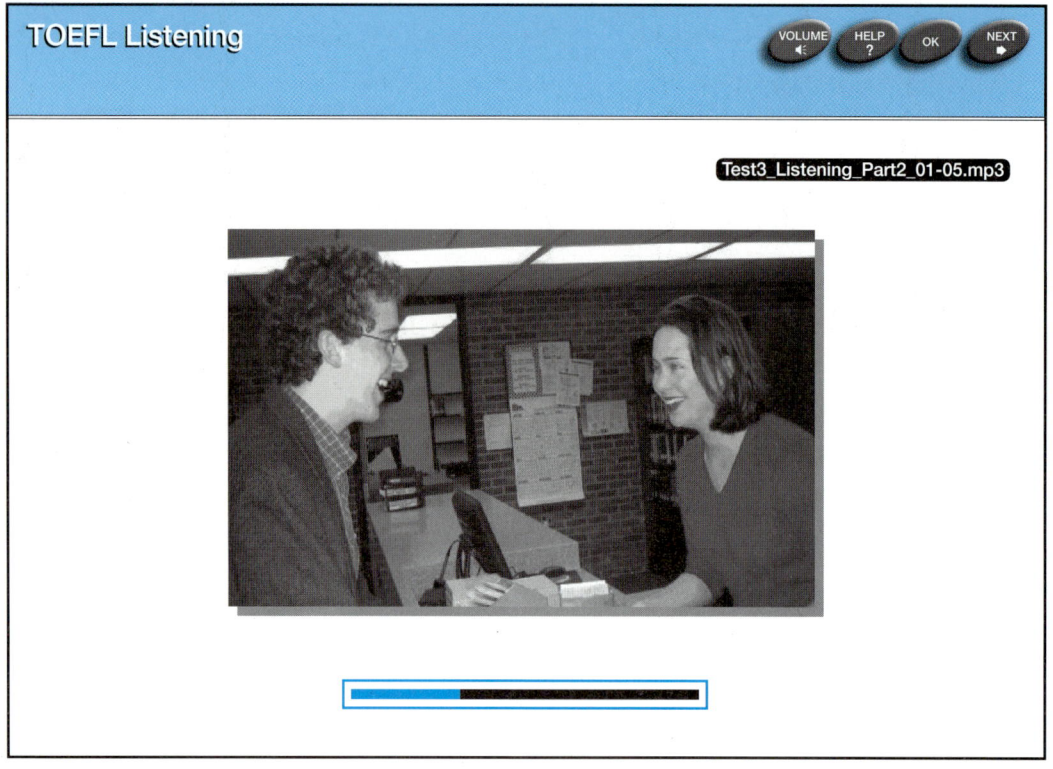

1. For what purpose does the student visit the clerk at the bookstore?
   Ⓐ To see which bookstores carry the textbook that he wants to buy
   Ⓑ To request help for finding a textbook for his computer science class
   Ⓒ To ask for directions to the computer bookstore
   Ⓓ To register for additional orders of the book

2. What is the student's initial assumption about why the particular textbook is missing at the bookstore?
   Ⓐ The course that uses the textbook is not part of the university's academic course.
   Ⓑ The course for the book is an advanced level.
   Ⓒ It is a computer related textbook, which is found in the computer bookstore.
   Ⓓ The course he is taking is only offered to the graduate student.

3. Why does the student need to purchase this textbook?
   Ⓐ Because the book is a requirement for a class
   Ⓑ Because there will soon be a mid-term exam on the book
   Ⓒ Because the professor already gave out the task on the material
   Ⓓ Because the book is unavailable due to a shortage

4. What does the woman mean when she says this:
   Ⓐ She is unable to assist the man any further.
   Ⓑ She is not sure she understands the man's question.
   Ⓒ She is somewhat certain the shipping time will be too long.
   Ⓓ She is uncertain about the length of the delivery.

Listen again to a part of the conversation. Then answer the question.

5. What is the clerk's main purpose when she asks:
   Ⓐ To clarify the correct spelling of the name of the professor
   Ⓑ To confirm that she is referring to the appropriate professor
   Ⓒ To ask for the spelling of the textbook author's name
   Ⓓ To convey that she has never heard of such a professor

[Questions 6-11] Listen to part of a lecture in an environmental science class.

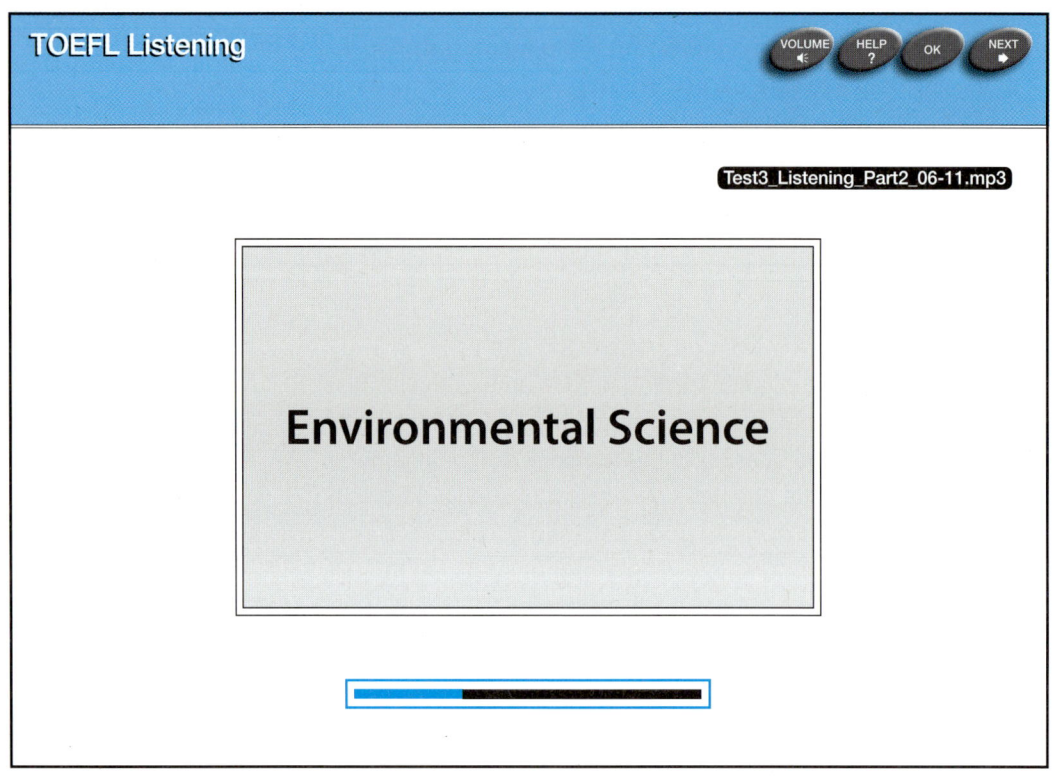

6. What is the main topic of the lecture?
   Ⓐ The factors that have an influence on a weather phenomenon
   Ⓑ The functional role of certain microorganisms regarding clouds
   Ⓒ The difference between various functions of the low thick clouds and high thin clouds
   Ⓓ The numerous effects and influences of the solar radiation on Earth

7. According to the professor, how does the albedo help keep track of the radiation budget of the Earth?
   Ⓐ It shows the ratio at which the surface of the Earth reflects and absorbs solar energy.
   Ⓑ It provides mathematical formula for calculating the numerical value of the radiation budget.
   Ⓒ It represents the percentage of solar energy reflection of a certain type of a surface.
   Ⓓ It is a device that captures the amount of solar energy reflection that a surface exerts.

8. For which two reasons do the high thin clouds contribute to the Earth's heating?
   Click on 2 answers.
   Ⓐ They are transparent to sunlight and are easily penetrated.
   Ⓑ They tend to capture the solar energy's heat.
   Ⓒ They produce a chemical called a dimethyl sulfide that increases the climate temperature.
   Ⓓ They block the heat that is exerted by the Earth out into the space.

9. Which of the following is true about the low thick clouds?
   Ⓐ It blocks most of the heat going out of the Earth and contributes to the cooling effect.
   Ⓑ It reflects the heat that comes into the Earth and contributes to cooling effect.
   Ⓒ It is not transparent to the sunlight and blocks all the light trying to reach the Earth.
   Ⓓ It causes the formation of the dimethyl sulfide produced by a certain marine plant.

10. What can be inferred about the marine plants that produce dimethyl sulfide?
   Ⓐ It is currently being harvested by scientists to control the weather on Earth.
   Ⓑ It is affecting high thin cloud formation by accelerating low thick cloud formation.
   Ⓒ It is the primary cause for the formation of low thick clouds around the world.
   Ⓓ It has the potential for practical scientific application to adjust the radiation budget.

11. Why does the professor say this:

Ⓐ To correct a common misconception

Ⓑ To discourage students from guessing

Ⓒ To highlight the potential of marine plants over land plants

Ⓓ To encourage students to share their opinion

[Questions 12-17] Listen to part of a lecture in a dance history class.

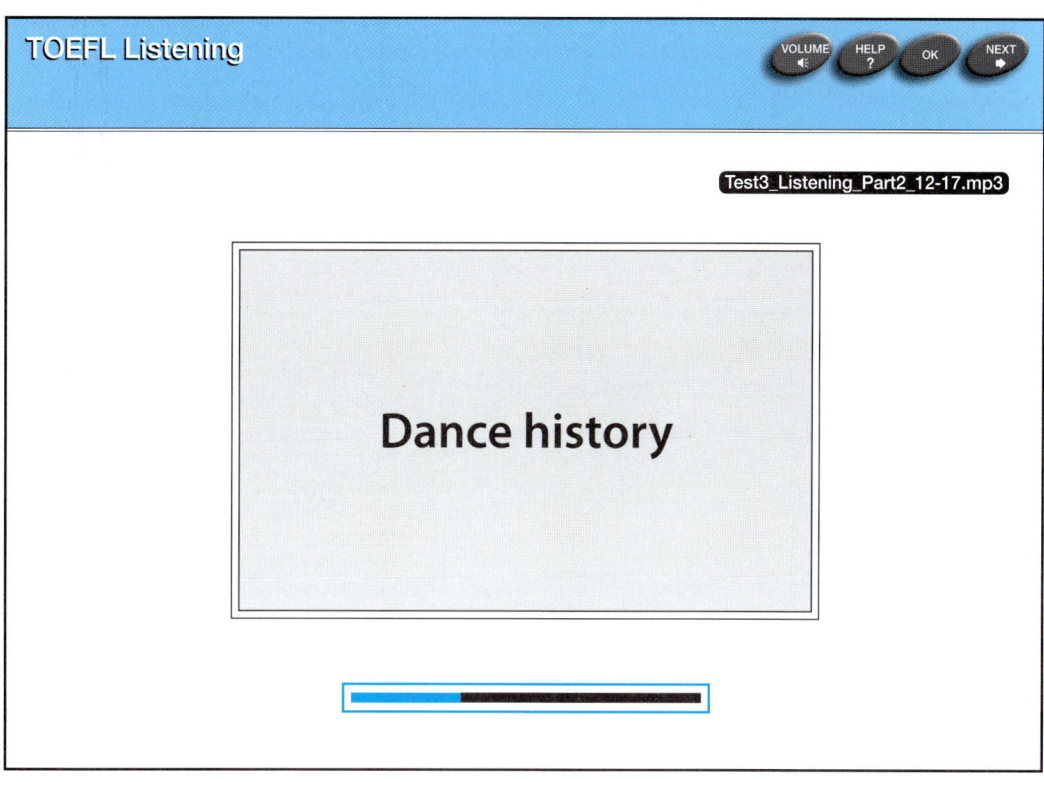

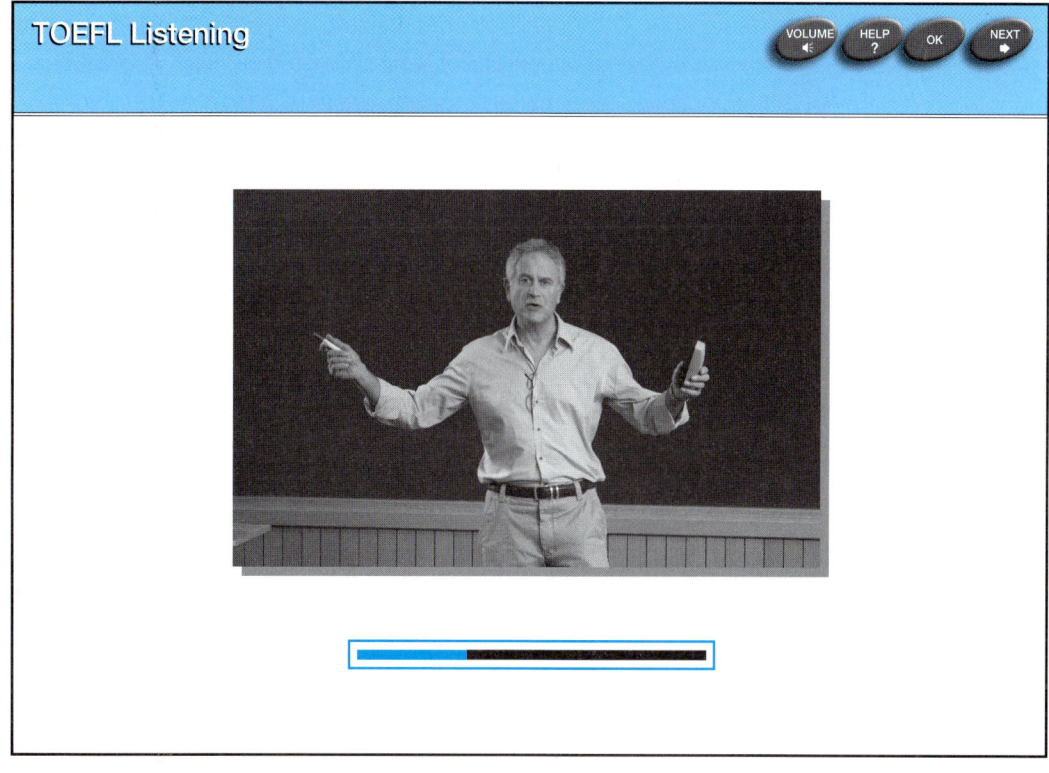

12. What is the lecture mainly about?
    Ⓐ How classical ballet originated from modern dance and music
    Ⓑ The difference between modern dances and classical ballet
    Ⓒ The characteristics of a certain type of performance
    Ⓓ The general public's reaction to modern dances

13. According to the professor, what can be inferred about modern dances at their
    early stage?
    Ⓐ They expressed inner emotions freely.
    Ⓑ They required a high level of improvisation.
    Ⓒ They were closely related to contemporary art.
    Ⓓ They shared similar artistic characteristics with classical ballet.

14. According to the lecture, what was the difference between classical ballet and
    modern dances?
    Ⓐ Unlike classical ballet, modern dance's expressive gestures were derived from
       strict techniques.
    Ⓑ Modern dances were greatly praised in France while classical ballet was decried
       in Russia.
    Ⓒ Modern dancers wore more free and loose clothing than the classical ballerinas
       did.
    Ⓓ Modern dances are physically less tiresome than classical ballet.

15. Why did Duncan dislike ballet? Click on 2 answers.
    Ⓐ The ballet technique seemed too strained and uncreative.
    Ⓑ Duncan viewed ballet as a hard and painful form of art.
    Ⓒ Duncan failed as a ballerina during her child hood.
    Ⓓ She personally disliked Pavlova who was a strong figure in the field of ballet.

16. For what purpose does the professor mention Ana Pavlova?
    Ⓐ To introduce Duncan's childhood rival when she did ballet
    Ⓑ To provide an example of a person who advocated the modern dances
    Ⓒ To describe how the competition between modern dances and classical ballet
       started
    Ⓓ To emphasize a leading figure of classical ballet in Russia

Listen again to a part of the conversation. Then answer the question.

17. What does the professor mean when he says:

      Ⓐ Comparatively speaking, Russian critics tend to be very harsh and critical in their reviews.

      Ⓑ Russian critics were not fond of a foreigner performing in their own country.

      Ⓒ Russians critics could not refrain from swooning over Duncan's performance.

      Ⓓ Russian critics denounced performance that went against their taste.

Speaking

Test3_Speaking_0_Direction.mp3

Speaking Section Directions

In this section of the test, you will be able to demonstrate your ability to speak about a variety of topics. You will answer six questions by speaking into the microphone. Answer as thoroughly as possible.

In questions 1 and 2, you will speak about familiar topics. Your response will be scored on your ability to speak clearly and coherently about the topics.

In questions 3 and 4, you will first read a short text. You will then listen to a talk on the same topic. You will need to combine appropriate information from the text and the talk to provide a complete answer to the question. Your response will be scored on your ability to speak clearly and coherently about what you have read and heard.

In questions 5 and 6, you will listen to part of a conversation or a lecture. You will then be asked a question about what you heard. Your response will be scored on your ability to speak clearly and coherently about what you have heard.

You may take notes while you read and while you listen to the conversations and lectures. You may use your notes to help prepare your response.

Listen carefully to the directions for each question. The directions will not be written on the screen.

For each question you will be given a short time to prepare your response. A clock will show how much preparation time is remaining. When the preparation time is up, you will be told to begin your response. A clock will show how much response time is remaining. A message will appear on the screen when the response time has ended.

Speaking

Test3_Speaking_1.mp3

Which of the following activities do you think is most beneficial for a child's growth?
- Playing sports
- Talking with elders of the community
- Traveling
Include specific examples and details to explain your answer.

Preparation Time
00 : 00 : 15 seconds

Response Time
00 : 00 : 45 seconds

VOLUME

Test3_Speaking_2.mp3

Do you agree or disagree with the following statement? People do not need to memorize historical events or references because they can now readily find such information from the Internet. Explain why. Use specific examples and details to support your answer.

Preparation Time
00 : 00 : 15 seconds

Response Time
00 : 00 : 45 seconds

Speaking

Test3_Speaking_3.mp3

Reading Time: 45 seconds

Banning Posters on School Walls

The school has been making an effort to improve the appearance of the campus by working on the gardens and cleaning out the buildings. However, despite the school's efforts, there does not seem to be much of an improvement due to all kinds of posters on the campus walls. Therefore, the school has decided to ban students from putting up posters on the walls. We will make a separate bulletin board in the dining hall for advertising events on campus. Students who want to advertise their clubs should use the school website. We will be making a separate link on the website for advertising clubs.

TOEFL Speaking

The woman expresses her opinion about the announcement on banning posters on the walls. State her opinion and explain the reasons why she feels that way.

Preparation Time
00 : 00 : 30 seconds

Response Time
00 : 00 : 60 seconds

Test3_Speaking_4.mp3

Reading Time: 45 seconds

Color Defense

Color defense is a defense mechanism that animals and insects use to defend themselves from predators. There are different types of color defense. One type is having the animal's body to have a similar color to its background. Another type of color defense is the opposite of the former method. Some animals have bright colors or patterns on their bodies. By standing out from the surrounded environment, they are able to warn predators and remind them that they are capable of attacking or defending themselves. Both of these methods of color defense are very effective in protecting animals from predators.

TOEFL Speaking

Using points and examples from the lecture, discuss what color defense is.

Preparation Time
00 : 00 : 30 seconds

Response Time
00 : 00 : 60 seconds

Speaking

Test3_Speaking_5.mp3

The woman expresses her feelings about the problem. What is the problem and what are the suggestions that are made? What do you think the woman should do?

Preparation Time
00 : 00 : 20 seconds

Response Time
00 : 00 : 60 seconds

Test3_Speaking_6.mp3

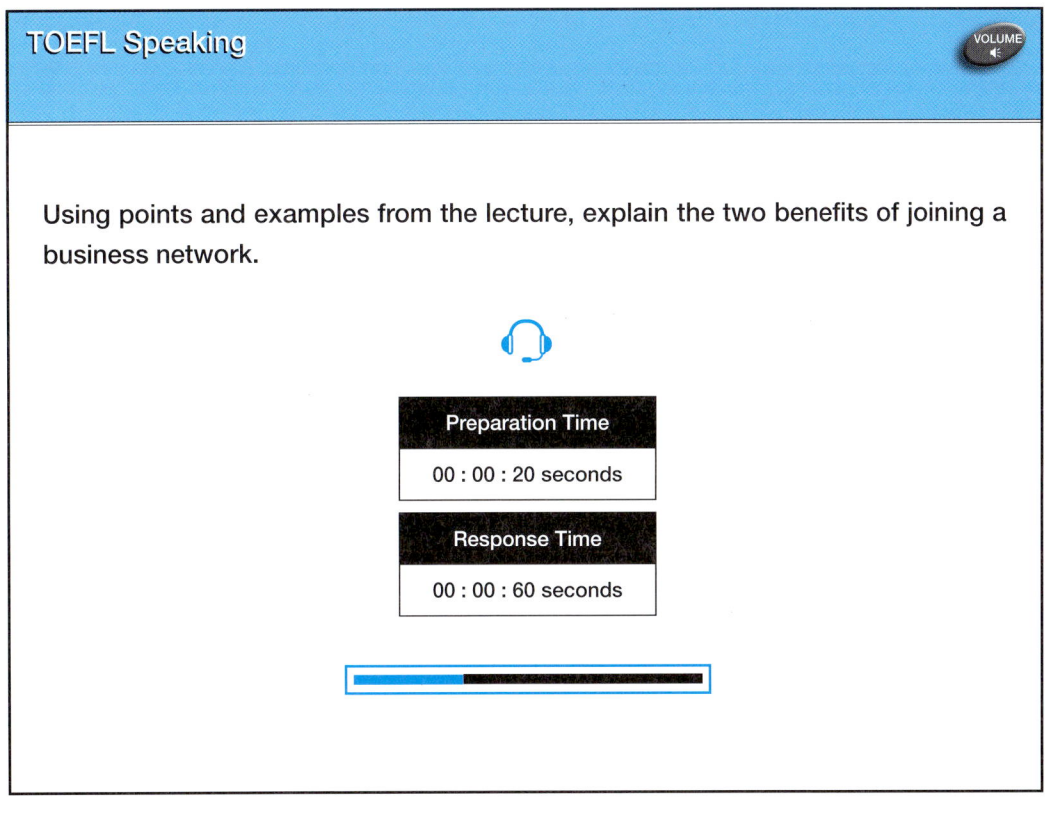

TOEFL Speaking

Using points and examples from the lecture, explain the two benefits of joining a business network.

Preparation Time

00 : 00 : 20 seconds

Response Time

00 : 00 : 60 seconds

Writing

Writing Section Directions

Be sure your headset is on.

This section measures your ability to write in an academic environment.

There are two tasks in this section. For the first task, there is a reading passage and a lecture. You will write a response to a question based on what you read and hear. For the second task, you will write a response to a question based on your own knowledge and experience.

Now, listen to the directions for the first writing task.

Writing

Reading Time: 3 minutes

Recent studies have shown that too much folic acid, also known as vitamin B, can be dangerous to the human body. Although folic acid is normally essential to human health as folic acid is responsible for producing healthy cells, like with anything else, too much folic acid can be hazardous. High amounts of folic acid can cause many health problems, especially amongst the elderly.

First of all, scientists have shown that high doses of folic acid can result in many harmful diseases including cancer. Less serious side effects include digestive problems, nausea and loss of appetite as the toxicity of folic acid is relatively low in comparison to other vitamins and minerals. However, if high amounts of folic acid in the body persist, problems can worsen quickly.

Also, high amounts of folic acid can be particularly harmful to elders. As older people need a good balance of vitamins and minerals to stay healthy, an overdose of folic acid can magnify the symptoms mentioned above, disrupting the intake of other vitamins. This could further complicate problems as they would not be getting other vitamins they need.

One method to control the amount of intake of folic acid is to use vitamins instead of food to get the right amount of folic acid. This is because it is easier to control the amount of folic acid one intakes when using vitamins instead of food. Therefore one should depend on vitamins for their daily intake of folic acid.

TOEFL Writing

PAUSE TEST SECTION EXIT

Task 1_Listening
Question 1 of 2

VOLUME HELP ? NEXT

HIDE TIME

Test3_Writing.mp3

Writing

Note-taking

	Reading	Listening
Main Argument		
Main Point 1		
Main Point 2		
Main Point 3		

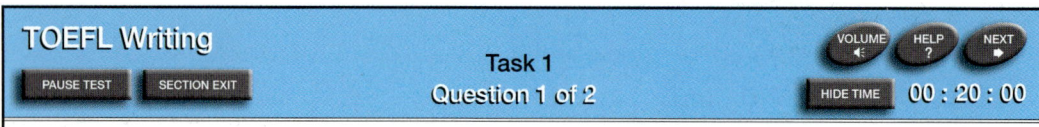

TOEFL Writing

PAUSE TEST   SECTION EXIT

Task 1
Question 1 of 2

VOLUME   HELP ?   NEXT

HIDE TIME   00 : 20 : 00

Directions: You have 20 minutes to plan and write your response. Your response will be judged on the basis of the quality of your writing and on how well your response presents the points in the lecture and the relationship to the reading passage. Typically, an effective response will be 150 to 225 words.

Question: Summarize the points made in the lecture, being sure to explain how they cast doubt on specific points made in the reading passage.

Copy   Paste   Undo   Redo   Word Count : 0

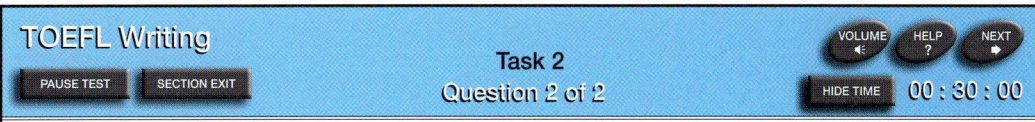

TOEFL Writing

PAUSE TEST   SECTION EXIT

Task 2
Question 2 of 2

VOLUME   HELP   NEXT
?

HIDE TIME   00 : 30 : 00

Directions: Read the question below. You have 30 minutes to plan, write, and revise your essay. Typically, an effective response will contain a minimum of 300 words.

Question:

Question: Do you agree or disagree with the following statement?

Cars (automobiles) have had a greater effect on society than planes have

Use specific reasons and examples to support your opinion.

Brainstorming

Writing

TOEFL Writing

PAUSE TEST   SECTION EXIT

Task 2
Question 2 of 2

VOLUME   HELP   NEXT
?

HIDE TIME   00 : 30 : 00

Copy   Paste   Undo   Redo

Word Count : 0

Reading

Part 1　The effect of steam engine

1. ⓒ	2. ⓒ	3. ⓓ	4. ⓑ	5. ⓒ	6. ⓒ	7. ⓒ
8. ⓒ	9. ⓓ	10. ⓓ	11. ⓒ	12. ⓐ	13. ⓑ	14. ⓐ, ⓔ, ⓕ

1 The **unprecedented** advancement of industry, technology, and economy known as the Industrial Revolution, and the factors of its realization, has been a source of debate among historians. Most technology before the 1700's was human or animal power-based but later developments harnessed the power of wind or water, which was highly beneficial for sailing and milling. Despite this technological growth, firewood was the main source of energy which was limited to its finite supply. Because of this factor, the Great Britain quickly ran out of **available** wood and faced an energy crisis. Coal, however, was available in large amounts under water, but there were no mechanized tools or machines that could be used to reach it. The steam engine would be the answer to this problem.

1 산업혁명으로 알려진 산업, 기술, 경제의 전례 없는 발전은 그것을 실현으로 이끈 요인들에 관해서 역사학자들 간에 논쟁의 원천이 되어 왔다. 1700년대 이전의 대부분의 기술은 인간과 동물의 힘을 기반으로 했지만, 나중에는 풍력과 수력을 동력으로 이용하게 되었고, 이것은 항해와 제분에 무척 유익했다. 이러한 기술적인 성장에도 불구하고 목재는 에너지의 주요한 원천이었지만 공급이 제한적이었다. 이러한 요인 때문에, 영국은 이용할 수 있는 나무를 빠르게 다 써버렸고, 에너지 위기에 직면하게 되었다. 그러나 석탄은 수중에서 대량으로 얻을 수 있었지만, 그것에 도달할 수 있도록 하는 기술적 도구나 기계가 없었다. 증기기관은 이러한 에너지 문제에 대한 해결책이 되었다.

2 The first commercially available steam engine was invented and developed by James Watt at the turn of the 18th century which was affordable and effective. The mining industry was the first to espouse this new steam engine, using it to pump out groundwater from coal mines in order for miners to more **contentedly** reach the coal. The engines also allowed mills to function away from large moving bodies of water, which augmented the overall flexibility and efficiency in the location of mills. For example, a wheat mill could be built right next to a field of wheat. Furthermore, the addition of a rotary motor on the steam engines could connect the shafts used to drive machines. This increased the use of steam engines to various other industries including the cotton

2 상업적으로 이용 가능했던 첫 번째 증기기관은 18세기 초반에 제임스 와트에 의해 만들어졌는데, 가격이 적당했고 효율적이기도 했다. 광업은 이러한 증기기관을 이용한 첫 번째 산업이었고, 광부들이 증기기관을 사용하여 석탄을 더 많이 얻기 위해 광산으로부터 지하수를 뽑아내었다. 이 증기기관은 또한 제분소가 흐르는 거대한 물줄기로부터 멀리 떨어져서 작동할 수 있도록 했으며, 이것은 제분소 위치의 전체적인 유동성과 효율성을 증대시켰다. 예를 들어, 제분소는 밀밭 바로 옆에 지어질 수 있었다. 게다가 증기기관의 추가 회전 모터는 기계를 돌리는 데 사용되는 수갱을 연결할 수 있었다. 이것은 면 산업 같은 여러 산업에 증기

industry. Evidence for the effectiveness of the use of steam engines in the cotton industry can be seen in Britain's exponential growth of cotton output during this time. As a result, cloth made of cotton accounted for a considerable amount of Britain's international commerce. From the mid 1700's to the mid 1800's cotton exports multiplied by 230, a sixty fold increase in overall output. This totaled up to half of Britain's total exports.

3 Steam engines found many uses in a variety of industries. The introduction of steam engines improved productivity and technology, and allowed the creation of smaller and better engines. After the high-pressure engines were developed, transport-applications became possible, and steam engines found their way into railways, farms and road vehicles. Ⓐ ▪ Steam engines are an example of how changes brought by industrialization led to even more changes in other areas. The iron industry also was benefitted by the invention of the steam engine. Ⓑ ▪ Before the steam engine, charcoal, a form of burnt wood, was the main source of fuel for iron furnaces. However, as supply of charcoal could not meet the demand, coke as a replacement (because of the reduced cost) the iron industry helped to improve. Ⓒ ▪ Steam powered bellows with this material were quickly implemented within all corners of the iron industry, and output in iron radically increased. By 1850 the Great Britain produced more iron than the rest of the world combined. Ⓓ ▪

4 The railroad industry was born from the developments of the steam engine and iron, further entrenching and lengthening the Industrial Revolution. Up to this point, shipping heavy loads of freight across large distances was extremely expensive despite developments in canals and roads. Heavy loads carried out of mines were mostly done through the use of horsepower using parallel railroads. The steam locomotive usurped

기관의 사용을 증진시켰다. 면 산업에서 증기기관의 사용 효용성에 대한 증거는 이 시기 동안에 영국의 면 산출량의 엄청난 증가에서 볼 수 있다. 그 결과로 면에 기초한 직물이 영국 국제무역의 중요한 부분이 되었다. 1700년 중반에서 1800년대 중반까지 면의 수출량은 230배 증가하였고, 전체 산출량은 60배가 늘었다. 이것은 영국 총 수출의 절반을 차지했다.

3 증기기관은 다양한 산업에서 많은 용도를 찾았다. 증기기관의 도입은 생산성과 기술을 향상시켰고, 더 작고 더 나은 엔진의 발명을 가능하게 했다. 높은 압력의 엔진이 개발된 후, 차량 적용이 가능해졌고, 증기기관은 철도, 농장, 그리고 도로주행 차량으로 보급되었다. 이것은 증기기관이 서로 다른 분야에서 훨씬 더 많은 변화를 이끈 산업화를 어떻게 가져왔는지에 대한 한 예이다. 제철 산업 또한 증기기관의 발명에 의해 이득을 보았다. 증기기관 이전에는, 탄 나무 형태인 숯이 제철 용광로의 주 연료였다. 그러나 숯의 공급이 수요를 충족시킬 수 없었기 때문에 (비용 절감 때문에) 코크스(석탄으로 만든 연료)가 제철 산업에서 (공급) 향상을 돕기 위한 대체제로 사용되었다. 이 연료와 함께 증기 벨로즈(풀무)는 빠르게 제철 산업의 모든 분야에서 사용되었으며, 철의 산출량도 빠르게 증가하였다. 1850년에 영국은 나머지 세계 합산량보다 더 많은 양의 철을 생산했다.

4 철도 산업은 증기기관과 철의 발달로 탄생되었고, 게다가 산업혁명을 훨씬 깊이 자리잡게 하고 길게 연장시켰다. 이때까지만 해도 먼 거리로 무거운 화물을 운반하는 것은 운하와 육로의 발전이 있었음에도 불구하고 굉장히 많은 비용이 들었다. 광산으로부터 나온 무거운 짐들은 주로 평행 선로를 이용한 마력을 통해 대부분 운반되었다. 증기기관차는 수송업을 장악했다. 기차는 무거운 화물들을

the transportation industry. Trains offered low-priced and fast procedures of transporting heavy loads of freight to reach far-away markets. The demand from the far away markets made the factories produce a myriad of products. Furthermore, profits made from the railroad industry were re-invested into other technologies and businesses. Low-skill laborers were needed to build these factories and tracks, year-round instead of seasonally. This resulted in an influx of peoples moving into larger cities to join this demographic increase.

꽤 멀리 떨어진 시장까지 빠르고 싸게 운반하는 것을 가능하게 했다. 멀리 있는 시장의 수요는 공장이 많은 제품들을 만들도록 했다. 게다가 철도 산업이 만들어낸 수익은 다른 기술과 산업에 재투자되었다. 기술이 별로 없는 노동자들이 공장과 철도를 건설하기 위해서 한때가 아닌, 연중 내내 필요했다. 이것은 더 큰 도시로 사람들이 유입되는 결과를 가져왔고 인구 증가에 한몫을 했다.

어휘_ unprecedented 전례 없는 fascinating 매력적인 adjacent 근처의, 총체적인 alternatives 대안 finite 유한한, 한정된 affordable 감당할 수 있는, 알맞은 mill 제분기 exponentially 굉장히 exclusively 배타적으로, 단독으로 extrinsic 외재적인 contentedly 만족하여 flexibility 유연성 output 결과 furnace 가마 replacement 대체 charcoal 숯 radically 굉장히 amplify 증대시키다 entrench 단단히 자리잡다 lengthen 늘이다 a myriad of 많은 render ~하게 만들다 influx 유입 catalyze 촉매화시키다 incite 선동하다

1. The word unprecedented in the passage is closest in meaning to
   Ⓐ prevailing
   Ⓑ fascinating
   Ⓒ novel
   Ⓓ thorough

지문의 단어 unprecedented와 의미가 가장 가까운 것은?
   Ⓐ 널리 퍼져 있는
   Ⓑ 매력적인
   Ⓒ 전례 없는
   Ⓓ 철저한

2. According to paragraph 1, before the 1700's the course of energy for a majority of the machines was
   Ⓐ the waste produced by humans and animals
   Ⓑ huge technological leaps in wind and water energy
   Ⓒ mainly through non-mechanical sources
   Ⓓ using wood cut from adjacent areas as a source of fuel

단락 1에 따르면, 1700년대 이전에 기계 대부분이 에너지원은 ~이었다.
   Ⓐ 사람과 동물에 의해 만들어진 폐기물
   Ⓑ 바람과 물 에너지의 굉장한 기술적인 도약
   Ⓒ 주로 비기계적인 자원을 통해서
   Ⓓ 연료의 원천으로 주변 지역에서 나온 자른 나무를 사용함

3. The word available in the passage is closest in meaning to
   Ⓐ profuse
   Ⓑ valuable
   Ⓒ infinite
   Ⓓ reachable

지문의 단어 available와 의미가 가장 가까운 것은?
   Ⓐ 풍부한
   Ⓑ 가치있는
   Ⓒ 무한한
   Ⓓ 얻을 수 있는

4. According to paragraph 1, before the 1700's Britain's perilous energy situation was made because
   Ⓐ technology was not developed enough to use renewable energy sources
   Ⓑ overuse of traditional forms of energy was a culprit
   Ⓒ sufficient amount of trees were planted to burn for fuel
   Ⓓ there were no alternatives to support energy supply

단락 1에 따르면, 1700년대 이전에 영국의 아주 위험한 에너지 상황은 ～ 때문에 발생했다.
   Ⓐ 기술은 재생 에너지원을 사용할 만큼 충분히 발달하지 않았기
   Ⓑ 전통적 형태의 에너지가 과다 사용이 되었기
   Ⓒ 충분한 양의 나무가 연료로 태우기 위해 심어졌기
   Ⓓ 에너지 공급을 뒷받침할 만한 대안이 없었기

5. Which of the following is true about steam engine in the paragraph 2?
   Ⓐ It reduced the cost of the coal production.
   Ⓑ It halted the exploitation of coal mines.
   Ⓒ It solved the problem with the groundwater.
   Ⓓ It could drill the ground, grind the soil and reach the deepest part in the ground.

단락 2에서 다음 중 어떤 것이 증기기관에 대해 사실인가?
   Ⓐ 증기기관은 석탄 생산 비용을 절감시켰다.
   Ⓑ 증기기관은 석탄 광산 개발을 금지했다.
   Ⓒ 증기기관은 지하수 문제를 해결했다.
   Ⓓ 증기기관은 땅에 구멍을 뚫고 토양을 갈고 땅의 가장 깊은 부분에 도달할 수 있었다.

6. The word contentedly in the passage is closest in meaning to
   Ⓐ comprehensively
   Ⓑ reasonably
   Ⓒ satisfactorily
   Ⓓ identically

지문의 단어 contentedly와 의미가 가장 가까운 것은?
   Ⓐ 완전히
   Ⓑ 상당히
   Ⓒ 만족하게
   Ⓓ 동등하게

7. What can be inferred about the building of mills after the introduction of the steam engine?
   Ⓐ Steam engines made the cotton industry the most crucial industry in the Great Britain.
   Ⓑ Bodies of water were no longer desired to power mills.
   Ⓒ The placement of mill depended less on location than in the past.
   Ⓓ Mills powered by steam engines had a larger output in creating goods than traditional mills due to more power.

증기기관의 도입 이후 제분소의 건설에 대해 추론할 수 있는 것은?
   Ⓐ 증기기관은 면 산업을 영국에서 가장 중요한 산업으로 만들었다.
   Ⓑ 물줄기가 더 이상 제분소를 동력화시키는 데 필요하지 않았다.
   Ⓒ 제분소의 배치는 과거보다는 장소에 덜 의존하게 되었다.
   Ⓓ 증기기관에 의해 운용되는 제분소는 더 많은 힘을 가지고 있어서 전통적인 제분소보다 더 많은 결과물을 만들어 내었다.

8. In paragraph 2, why does the author mention the cotton industry?
   Ⓐ To suggest the popularity of the engine in Britain
   Ⓑ To show Britain's strength in the particular business
   Ⓒ To show the effectiveness of the steam engines
   Ⓓ To state the success of Britain's cotton industry to be responsible for half of all its exports

단락 2에서, 필자는 왜 면 산업에 대해서 언급하는가?
   Ⓐ 영국에서 엔진의 인기를 말하기 위해서
   Ⓑ 특정한 산업에서 영국의 강점을 보여주기 위해서
   Ⓒ 증기기관의 효용성을 보여주기 위해서
   Ⓓ 영국 면 산업의 성공이 전체 수출의 절반을 책임진다는 것을 언급하기 위해서

9. The word considerable in the passage is closest in meaning to
   Ⓐ exceptional
   Ⓑ exclusive
   Ⓒ extrinsic
   Ⓓ substantial

지문의 단어 considerable과 의미가 가장 가까운 것은?
   Ⓐ 특출한
   Ⓑ 독점적인
   Ⓒ 외적인
   Ⓓ 상당한

10. Look at the four squares [■] that indicate where the following sentence can be added to the passage.

This is easily evident in the appreciable growth of the amount of iron produced by the country.

Where would the sentence best fit?

다음 문장이 지문의 어느 곳에 추가될 수 있는지를 나타내는 네 개의 정사각형을 보시오.

이것은 그 나라에서 생산된 철의 양의 상승에서 쉽게 명확해진다.

이 문장이 어디에 가장 적절하겠는가?

11. Which of the sentences below best expresses the most important information in the highlighted section of the passage? *Incorrect answer choices change the meaning in important ways or leave out essential information.*
   Ⓐ The Industrial Revolution would most likely have not been long and rooted in history if not for the steam engine's capacity to catalyze iron.
   Ⓑ The platform of the entrenchment and length of the Industrial Revolution was the steam engine's role in further expanding the railroad industry.

아래의 문장 중 어떤 것이 하이라이트된 지문의 가장 중요한 정보를 가장 잘 표현하는가? 오답을 선택하면 중요한 면에서 의미를 왜곡하거나 필수적인 정보를 누락시키게 된다.
   Ⓐ 산업혁명은 증기기관이 철을 촉매화시키는 능력이 없었더라면, 오래가지 못했거나 역사에 뿌리를 내리지 못했을 것이다.
   Ⓑ 산업혁명이 자리를 잡고 길게 유지될 수 있었던 기반은 철도 산업을 더 넓게 확장시킨 증기기관의 역할에 있다.

Ⓒ The growth of the railroad industry through the combined technologies of the steam engine and iron resulted in an increase in the importance of the Industrial Revolution.

Ⓓ The synthesis of the steam engine and iron independently played the key role in expansion of the railroad industry through the entrenched prolongation of the Industrial Revolution.

Ⓒ 철과 증기기관 기술의 결합을 통한 철도 산업의 성장은 산업혁명의 중요성을 증가 시켰다.

Ⓓ 증기기관과 철의 결합은 산업혁명의 확고 한 연장을 통해 철도 산업 확장에 독립적 으로 중요한 역할을 했다.

12. According to the paragraph 4, what caused an increase in the demand for goods made by factories?

Ⓐ Products could be moved over long distances with lower shipping costs than ever before.

Ⓑ The steam powered locomotive could move trains without using horses.

Ⓒ Trains gained the ability to carry much larger loads than ever before.

Ⓓ Consumers were allowed to have fresher products made possible.

단락 4에 따르면, 무엇이 공장에서 만들어진 상 품에 대한 수요를 증대시켰는가?

Ⓐ 상품들이 예전보다 더 낮은 운송비용으로 먼 거리까지 이동될 수 있었다.

Ⓑ 증기기관차는 말을 사용하지 않고 기차를 움직일 수 있었다.

Ⓒ 기차는 예전보다 더 많은 무게를 싣고 이 동할 수 있는 능력을 얻게 되었다.

Ⓓ 소비자들은 가능한 한 보다 신선한 상품들 을 가질 수 있게 되었다.

13. According to paragraph 4, which of the following did NOT happen after the invention of the steam locomotive?

Ⓐ Factories made a large amount of products in order to meet the steep increase of demand.

Ⓑ More railroads were built as fast as possible.

Ⓒ The working population increased in the cities.

Ⓓ Business opportunities opened up for railroad entrepreneurs in theirs and other industries.

단락 4에 따르면, 다음 중 어떤 것이 증기기관 의 발명 이후에 발생하지 않았는가?

Ⓐ 가파른 수요 증가를 충족시키기 위해 공장 은 다량의 상품을 생산했다.

Ⓑ 더 많은 기찻길이 만들어져서 상품들이 많 은 다른 지역으로 배달될 수 있었다.

Ⓒ 일하는 인구들이 다른 산업에 더 많이 고 용될 수 있는 기회를 얻었다.

Ⓓ 철도 사업가들에게 철도 산업과 다른 산업 에서의 산업 기회가 생겼다.

14. **Directions**: An introduction for a short summary of the passage appears below. Complete the summary by selecting the **THREE** answer choices that mention the most important points in the passage. Some sentences do not belong in the summary because they express ideas that are not presented in the passage or are minor ideas in the passage. **This question is worth 2 point.**

A shortfall of wood, which is Britain's primary source of fuel, forced Britain to find alternate sources of energy in the 18th century.

-
-
-

Ⓐ Coal became accessible as a result of the steam engine, opening up opportunities for many different industries at the time.

Ⓑ The rotary motor allowed the attachment of a steam engine and connecting roads that could be used to power machines in a wide spectrum of uses.

Ⓒ Replacing the older element of charcoal with coke allowed iron forges to forge higher quality iron in a vast assortment of mixtures inciting demand for iron products.

Ⓓ As Britain became the producer of more iron in the world than all other countries combined, iron industry was responsible for a huge section of Britain's international trade because of steam engines.

Ⓔ The transportation industry along with others grew exponentially with the invention of the steam engine.

Ⓕ The steam engine began to be used in many industrial settings and became one of the most important businesses of the Industrial Revolution and served as a kind of important factors for much of the British economy.

지문의 짧은 요약을 위한 소개문이 아래에 나와 있다. 지문에서 가장 중요한 요점을 나타내는 정답 3개를 선택해서 요약문을 완성하시오. 몇 몇 문장은 지문에 제시되지 않거나 중요하지 않 은 생각을 표현하기 때문에 요약에 포함되지 않 았다. 이 문제는 2점이다.

영국의 연료의 중요한 원천이었던 나무의 부족 이 영국으로 하여금 18세기에 다른 에너지원을 찾게 했다.

-
-
-

Ⓐ 석탄은 증기기관의 결과로 접근할 수 있게 되었고, 당시에 많은 다양한 산업에 기회를 열어주었다.

Ⓑ 회전 모터는 증기기관의 부착을 가능하게 했고, 다양한 사용에 있어서 기계에 동력으 로 사용되는 길을 연결했다.

Ⓒ 오래된 연료인 숯을 코크스로 대치시키는 것은 제철소가 여러 혼합물에서 양질의 철 을 만들 수 있게 하여 철제품의 수요를 자 극했다.

Ⓓ 영국이 모든 다른 나라들을 합한 것보다 전 세계에서 더 많은 철의 생산자가 되자, 철 산업은 증기기관 덕분에 영국의 국제 무역에서 상당 부분 책임을 졌다.

Ⓔ 증기기관차로 이어진 증기기관이 발명으로 운송 산업은 다른 산업들과 어울려 기하급 수적으로 성장했다.

Ⓕ 증기기관은 많은 산업 환경에서 사용되기 시작했고, 산업혁명의 가장 중요한 사업이 되었으며 영국 경제의 많은 부분에서 중요 한 요인으로서 역할을 했다.

Part 2 Magma

1. Ⓓ	2. Ⓑ	3. Ⓐ	4. Ⓑ	5. Ⓓ	6. Ⓑ	7. Ⓑ
8. Ⓒ	9. Ⓒ	10. Ⓒ	11. Ⓑ	12. Ⓑ	13. Ⓐ	14. Ⓐ, Ⓒ, Ⓓ

1 Some magma actions are different from that of other magma. Why does one type of magma behave so differently from other? The basic perception is that as magma is a liquid rock, its density is lower than that of the rock around **it**, which magma to rise upwards. There are two distinct changes. One change is that magma's temperature decreases as it ascends away from the center of the Earth. Another change is that pressure on magma also decreases as there it rises since the rock pressing down on the magma becomes less in amounts; as a result, it causes the magma to rise even faster than before. These two changes occurring at the same time have contrasting effects on magma. Solidification occurs for reason that magma cools as it rises away from the core. Yet the temperature of magma will increase caused by less pressure imposed on magma, which keeps magma liquid.

1 몇몇 마그마 활동은 다른 마그마 활동과 다르다. 왜 한 종류의 마그마가 다른 것들과 그렇게 다를까? 기본적인 개념은 마그마가 액상의 암석이라는 것이고, 이것의 밀도가 주위 암석의 밀도보다 낮아서 마그마가 위로 올라간다는 것이다. 두 가지 눈에 띄는 변화가 있다. 한 가지 변화는 마그마가 지구의 중심부로부터 멀어져 올라갈 때 마그마의 온도가 떨어진다는 것이다. 또 다른 변화는 마그마가 상승함에 따라 마그마에 가해지는 압력도 또한 감소한다는 것인데, 이는 마그마를 억누르는 암석이 양적으로 적어지기 때문이고, 그 결과 마그마는 전보다 훨씬 더 빨리 올라간다. 이렇게 동시에 일어나는 두 가지 변화는 마그마에 대조(對照) 효과를 준다. 마그마가 지구 중심부로부터 멀어지면서 냉각되기 때문에 고체화가 발생한다. 그러나 마그마의 온도는 마그마에 미치는 더 낮은 압력에 의해 증가할 것이고 이것은 마그마가 액체 상태가 되도록 할 것이다.

2 The behaviors of magma can be comprehended by looking into their compositions. All magma contains gases and a mixture of simple elements. Magma can be divided into mafic magma, intermediate magma or felsic magma. Oxygen and silicon are the most **abundant** elements in magma, and geologists define magma types in terms of their silica content. These differences in chemical composition are directly related to differences in gas content, temperature, and viscosity. Mafic magma has relatively low silica content, roughly 50%, and higher contents in iron and magnesium. This type of magma has a low gas content and low viscosity, or resistance to flow. Mafic magma also has high mean temperatures, between 1000° and 2000°. Low viscosity means that mafic

2. 마그마의 성질은 구성 성분을 살펴봄으로써 이해될 수 있다. 모든 마그마는 가스와 단순한 성분의 혼합물을 포함한다. 마그마는 유색 마그마(mafic magma), 안산암질 마그마(intermediate magma), 그리고 규장질 마그마(felsic magma)로 나눌 수 있다. 산소와 규소가 마그마에서 가장 풍부한 성분이며, 지질학자들은 이산화규소의 함량 측면에서 마그마의 종류를 정의했다. 화학적 구성 성분의 이러한 차이들은 가스 함량, 온도, 점도의 차이와 직접적으로 연관된다. 유색 마그마는 대략 50% 정도로 비교적 낮은 이산화규소 함량과 더 높은 철과 마그네슘 함량을 지닌다. 이 유형의 미그마는 낮은 가스 함량과 낮은 점도 혹은 흐름 저항을 가지

magma is the most fluid of magma types. It erupts non-explosively and moves very quickly when it reaches Earth's surface as lava. This lava cools into basalt, a rock that is heavy and dark in color due to its higher iron and magnesium levels. Basalt is one of the most common rocks in Earth's crust as well as the volcanic islands created by hot spots. The Hawaiian Islands are a direct result of mafic magma eruptions.

3 Intermediate magma has higher silica content than mafic magma. This results in a higher gas content and viscosity. Its mean temperature ranges from 800° to 1000° Celsius. **As a result of its higher viscosity and gas content, intermediate magma builds up pressure below the Earth's surface before it can be released as lava.** This more gaseous and sticky lava tends to explode violently and cools as andesite rock. Intermediate magma most commonly transforms into andesite due to the transfer of heat at convergent plate boundaries. Andesitic rocks are often found at continent of volcanic arcs, such as the Andes Mountains in South America, after which they are named.

4 Felsic magma has the highest silica content of all magma types, between 65-70%. As a result, felsic magma also has the highest gas content and viscosity, and lowest mean temperatures, between 650° and 800° Celsius. Thick, viscous felsic magma can trap gas bubbles in a volcano's magma chamber. These trapped bubbles can cause explosive and destructive eruptions. These eruptions eject lava violently into the air, which cools into igneous, volcanic rock. Much like intermediate magma, felsic magma may be most commonly found at convergent plate boundaries where transfer of heat and flux melting create large stratovolcanoes.

고 있다. 유색 마그마는 또한 1,000도에서 2,000도의 높은 평균 온도를 갖는다. 낮은 점도는 유색 마그마가 대부분 유체의 마그마 종류임을 의미한다. 그것은 비폭발적이고 용암으로서 지각 위로 도달했을 때 매우 빨리 움직인다. 이 용암은 높은 수준의 철과 마그네슘 때문에 무겁고 어두운 색의 현무암으로 식는다. 현무암은 핫스팟으로부터 만들어진 화산섬뿐 아니라 지각에서도 가장 흔한 암석이다. 하와이 제도 또한 바로 유색 마그마의 폭발로 인한 직접적인 결과이다.

3 안산암질 마그마는 유색 마그마보다 높은 이산화규소 함량을 가지고 있다. 이 마그마는 높은 가스 함량과 점도를 갖게 한다. 이것의 평균 온도는 섭씨 800도에서 1,000도이다. 이러한 높은 점도와 가스 함량의 결과로 안산암질 마그마는 용암으로 분출되기 전에 지각 아래에서 압력을 축적한다. 이러한 더 많아진 기체 상태의 끈적이는 용암은 격렬하게 폭발하는 경향이 있고 안산암으로 식는다. 안산암질 마그마는 대부분 수렴 경계에서 열의 이동 때문에 보통 안산암으로 변형된다. 안산암은 종종 남아메리카의 안데스 산맥과 같은 화산호 모양의 대륙에서 발견되었고, 그 후에 이것을 따라 이름이 붙여졌다.

4 규장질 마그마는 65%에서 70%로 모든 마그마 종류 중 가장 높은 이산화규소 함량을 가지고 있다. 그 결과, 규장질 마그마는 또한 가장 높은 가스 함량과 점도와 섭씨 650도에서 800도의 가장 낮은 평균 온도를 가지고 있다. 두껍고 끈적거리는 규장질 마그마는 가스 거품을 화산 마그마류에 가둔다. 이렇게 갇힌 거품은 폭발적이고 파괴적인 폭발을 야기한다. 이러한 폭발은 화성의 화산암으로 식게 되는 용암을 공기 중에 격렬하게 분출시킨다. 안산암질 마그마와 유사하게, 규장질 마그마는 거대한 성층화산을 만드는 열과

유속 용해가 이동하는 수렴 경계에서 발견된다.

5 Another point to contemplate is what happens after the solidification takes place. Crystallized form is made from magma slowly cooling below the surface of the earth. Ⓐ ■ Plutons are much higher in density compared to that of the earth's crust. In practice, pluton usually refers to a distinctive mass of igneous rock, typically several kilometers in dimension. Ⓑ ■ Plutons can push through the crust due to the elasticity. Ⓒ ■ The foundation of the earth's crust is very boiling and it gets softer as the temperature rises and become rigid as it cools. So, the Plutons will push upwards underneath the crust where the rock is hot. Ⓓ ■

5 고려해야 할 또 다른 점은 응결이 일어난 뒤에 무엇이 발생하는가이다. 결정화된 형태는 지각의 표면 아래에서 천천히 냉각되면서 형성된다. 심성암은 지표면 아래에서 천천히 식어 마그마로부터 결정체를 이룬다. 심성암은 지각의 밀도보다 훨씬 높은 밀도를 가지고 있다. 실제로, 심성암은 종종 화성암의 일반적으로 수 킬로미터나 되는 규모의 독특한 덩어리를 나타낸다. 심성암은 탄성 때문에 지각을 밀고 나간다. 지각의 기반은 매우 덥고 온도가 상승함에 따라 부드러워지며 식으면서 단단해진다. 따라서 심성암은 암석이 뜨거운 곳의 지각 아래에서 밀고 올라갈 것이다.

어휘_ perception 인식 distinct 독특한 comprehend 이해하다 composition 구성요소 mafic magma 유색 마그마 intermediate magma 안산암질 마그마 felsic magma 규장질 마그마 in terms of ~의 면에서 content 함량 viscosity 점도 relatively 비교적 silica 이산화규소 roughly 대략 iron 철 magnesium 마그네슘 mean 평균의 fluid 유체 basalt 현무암 gaseous 기체의 sticky 끈적이는 explode 폭발하다 violently 격렬하게 andesite rock 안산암 transform 변형되다 transfer 이동 convergent plate boundary 수렴 경계 viscous 끈적거리는 trap 가두다 magma chamber 마그마류 destructive 파괴적인 eruption 폭발 igneous 화성의 flux melting 유속용해 solidification 응결 pluton 심성암 crystallize 결정체를 이루다 density 밀도 in practice 실제로 dimension 규모 push through 밀고 나가다 elasticity 탄성 foundation 기반 rigid 단단한

1. According to paragraph 1, what makes magma rise
   upward?
   Ⓐ The fact that there is differentiation between
      magma temperatures
   Ⓑ The fact that magma has a tendency to move freely
   Ⓒ An increased pressure exerted by the rock above
      the magma
   Ⓓ A characteristic property variation in magma and
      rock that surrounds the magma

단락 1에 따르면, 마그마를 위로 향하게 하는
것은 무엇인가?
   Ⓐ 마그마 온도 사이에 차이가 있다는 사실
   Ⓑ 마그마가 자유롭게 움직이는 경향이 있다
      는 사실
   Ⓒ 마그마 위의 바위로 인해 가해지는 증가된
      압력이 있다는 것
   Ⓓ 마그마를 둘러싼 마그마와 암석의 특징 있
      는 성질의 차이

2. The word it in paragraph 1 refers to
   Ⓐ rock
   Ⓑ magma
   Ⓒ liquid
   Ⓓ density

단락 1에서 it이 언급하는 것은?
   Ⓐ 바위
   Ⓑ 마그마
   Ⓒ 액체
   Ⓓ 밀도

3. The word abundant in the passage is closest in
   meaning to
   Ⓐ profuse
   Ⓑ enormous
   Ⓒ crucial
   Ⓓ impending

지문의 단어 abundant와 의미가 가장 가까운
것은?
   Ⓐ 많은
   Ⓑ 거대한
   Ⓒ 중대한, 결정적인
   Ⓓ 임박한

4. Why does the author mention Hawaiian island
   according to the paragraph 2?
   Ⓐ To show it is the only example of mafic magma
   Ⓑ To show it demonstrates mafic magma contents
   Ⓒ To show the Hawaiian island has cool lava
   Ⓓ To show it is one of the common rocks in earth

단락 2에서 작가는 왜 하와이 제도를 언급하는가?
   Ⓐ 그것이 유색 마그마의 단 하나의 예임을
      보여주기 위해서
   Ⓑ 그것이 유색 마그마의 구성 성분을 설명한
      다는 점을 보여주기 위해서
   Ⓒ 하와이 제도가 차가운 용암을 가지고 있다
      는 것을 보여주기 위해서
   Ⓓ 그것이 지구에서 가장 흔한 암석들 중 하
      나라는 것을 보여주기 위해서

5. According to paragraph 2, what can be inferred about silica content?

  Ⓐ The viscosity of the magma is chemical reaction of silica and the other elements.

  Ⓑ The speed of the magma is affected by the temperature of its silica and magnesium.

  Ⓒ Mafic magma is stiffer than felsic magma because of its movement.

  Ⓓ The amount of silica in magma determines the viscosity of magma.

단락 2에 따르면, 이산화규소 함량에 대해 추론할 수 있는 것은?

  Ⓐ 마그마의 점성은 이산화규소와 다른 성분들의 화학반응이다.

  Ⓑ 마그마의 속도는 이산화규소와 마그네슘의 온도에 의해 영향을 받는다.

  Ⓒ 유색 마그마는 움직임 때문에 규장질 마그마보다 더 단단하다.

  Ⓓ 마그마 속 이산화규소의 양은 마그마의 점성을 결정한다.

6. The word released in the passage is closest in meaning to

  Ⓐ infiltrated

  Ⓑ discharged

  Ⓒ percolated

  Ⓓ recharged

지문의 단어 released와 의미가 가장 가까운 것은?

  Ⓐ 침투하다

  Ⓑ 방출하다

  Ⓒ 스며들다

  Ⓓ 나오다

7. Which of the sentences below best expresses the most important information in the highlighted section of the passage? *Incorrect answer choices change the meaning in important ways or leave out essential information.*

  Ⓐ As intermediate magma releases lava, it increases the pressure below the earth's surface because of high thickness and gas content.

  Ⓑ Under the earth surface, intermediate magma increases pressure high with high viscosity and high gas contents and, then it is discharged as lava.

  Ⓒ Viscosity and gas content are the most crucial elements when intermediate magma builds up pressure.

  Ⓓ Intermediate magma can be discharged as lava when magma has high viscosity and high gas content.

아래의 문장 중 어떤 것이 하이라이트된 지문의 가장 중요한 정보를 가장 잘 표현하는가? 오답을 선택하면 중요한 면에서 의미를 왜곡하거나 필수적인 정보를 누락시키게 된다.

  Ⓐ 안산암질 마그마는 용암을 분출하면서, 높은 밀도와 가스의 함유량 때문에 지표면 아래쪽에 압력을 증가시킨다.

  Ⓑ 지표면 아래에서 안산암질 마그마는 높은 점도와 높은 가스의 함유량을 높이고 나서 용암으로 방출된다.

  Ⓒ 점도와 가스 함유량은 안산암질 마그마가 압력을 축적할 때 가장 중요한 요소이다.

  Ⓓ 안산암질 마그마는 마그마가 높은 점도와 높은 가스의 함유량을 가질 때 용암으로 방출될 수 있다.

8. According to the paragraph 2, 3, which of the following are NOT components which cause magma to divide into three groups?
   Ⓐ The behavior of magma is controlled by temperature.
   Ⓑ Resistance to flow determines characteristics of magma.
   Ⓒ The lava content determines how the magma behaves.
   Ⓓ Silica content in the rocks regulates the properties of magma.

단락 2, 3에 따르면, 다음 중 어떤 것이 마그마를 세 그룹으로 나누는 요소가 아닌가?
   Ⓐ 마그마의 성질은 온도에 의해 조절된다.
   Ⓑ 흐름에 대한 저항이 마그마의 성질을 결정한다.
   Ⓒ 용암의 함량이 마그마가 어떻게 반응하는지를 결정한다.
   Ⓓ 암석의 이산화규소 함량이 마그마의 특징을 규정한다.

9. According to paragraph 3, which of the following is true about andesitic rock?
   Ⓐ It was the source of the Andes Mountains' name.
   Ⓑ There is a tremendous pressure on the water from being squeezed into the andesitic rock.
   Ⓒ The movement of the heat makes convert to andesitic rock from intermediate magma.
   Ⓓ The downward force on the magma from the rock captures water contents within the andesitic rock.

단락 3에 따르면, 다음 중 어떤 것이 안산암질 암석에 대해 사실인가?
   Ⓐ 그것은 안데스 산맥의 이름의 원천이다.
   Ⓑ 안산암질 암석 속으로 빨려 들어가는 물에 가해지는 엄청난 압력이 있다.
   Ⓒ 열의 이동이 안산암질 마그마로부터 안산암질 암석으로 변화하도록 만든다.
   Ⓓ 암석으로부터 마그마에 아래쪽으로 가해지는 힘이 안산암질 암석 안에 물의 함량을 갖게 한다.

10. What can be inferred about felsic magma's behavior in paragraph 4?
   Ⓐ Felsic magma behaves more like a liquid than like a solid.
   Ⓑ Felsic magma has 1% or 2% water that plays significant role.
   Ⓒ Felsic magma is the magma seen in volcanic eruptions.
   Ⓓ Felsic magma has a much lower point of solidification than mafic magma.

다음 중 단락 4에서 규장질 마그마의 성격에 대해서 추론할 수 있는 것은?
   Ⓐ 규장질 마그마는 고체보다 기체에 가깝게 반응한다.
   Ⓑ 규장질 마그마는 중요한 역할을 하는 1%에서 2%의 물을 가진다.
   Ⓒ 규장질 마그마는 화산 폭발에서 볼 수 있는 마그마이다.
   Ⓓ 규장질 마그마는 유색 마그마보다 훨씬 낮은 응고점을 가진다.

11. The word contemplate in passage is closest in meaning to
   Ⓐ scrutinize
   Ⓑ speculate
   Ⓒ discourse
   Ⓓ attribute

지문의 단어 contemplate와 의미가 가장 가까운 것은?
   Ⓐ 세심히 살피다
   Ⓑ 추측하다
   Ⓒ 논하다
   Ⓓ 탓으로 돌리다

12. Which of the following is true about the pluton in paragraph 5?
   Ⓐ Pluton is the hard crystalized plate above the earth's crust.
   Ⓑ Pluton is formed when magma cools slowly.
   Ⓒ Pluton is the most critical component because of the elasticity.
   Ⓓ Pluton is a melted volcano which is several kilometers in height.

13. Look at the four squares [■] that indicate where the following sentence can be added to the passage.

The solidified magma formed below the earth's crust is called Plutons.

Where would the sentence best fit?

14. Directions: An introduction for a short summary of the passage appears below. Complete the summary by selecting the **THREE** answer choices that mention the most important points in the passage. Some sentences do not belong in the summary because they express ideas that are not presented in the passage or are minor ideas in the passage. **This question is worth 2 point.**

Magma is a mixture of molten rocks that is found beneath the surface of the Earth and is divided into different kinds.

-
-
-

   Ⓐ The specific proportions of minerals in the magma determine how the magma behaves.
   Ⓑ Mafic magma contains 50% silica content and its mean temperature is between 1000° and 2000° while Intermediate magma's mean temperature ranges from 800° to 1000°C.

단락 5에서 다음 중 어떤 것이 심성암에 대해 사실인가?
   Ⓐ 심성암은 지각 위에 단단하게 결정화된 판이다.
   Ⓑ 심성암은 마그마가 천천히 식을 때 형성된다.
   Ⓒ 심성암은 탄성 때문에 가장 중요한 요소이다.
   Ⓓ 심성암은 수 킬로미터 높이의 녹은 화산이다.

다음 문장이 지문의 어느 곳에 추가될 수 있는지를 나타내는 네 개의 정사각형을 보시오.

굳어진 마그마는 지각의 아래에서 형성되어 심성암이라고 불린다.

이 문장이 어디에 가장 적절하겠는가?

지문의 짧은 요약을 위한 소개문이 아래에 나와 있다. 지문에서 가장 중요한 요점을 나타내는 정답 3개를 선택해서 요약문을 완성하시오. 몇몇 문장은 지문에 제시되지 않거나 중요하지 않은 생각을 표현하기 때문에 요약에 포함되지 않았다. 이 문제는 2점이다.

마그마는 지표면 아래에서 형성된 녹은 암석의 혼합이며 여러 가지 종류로 나뉜다.

-
-
-

   Ⓐ 마그마 광물의 세부적 비율은 마그마가 어떻게 반응하는지를 결정한다.
   Ⓑ 유색 마그마는 50%의 이산화규소를 가지고 있고 평균 온도는 1,000도에서 2,000도인 반면 안산암질 마그마는 온도가 800도에서 1,000도 정도이다.

© Silicate in the magma determines the viscosity of the magma, which has a direct effect on how ease the magma move.

① Differences in chemical composition are directly related to differences in gas content, temperature, and viscosity.

② Mafic magma has more violent eruptions than felsic volcanoes since their properties enable them to act much like fluid.

② Mafic volcanoes are the most common and the Hawaiian Islands and they are the best example of places made by mafic magma.

© 마그마의 이산화규소는 마그마의 점도를 결정하고, 마그마가 얼마나 쉽게 움직이는지에 대해 직접적인 영향을 준다.

① 화학적 구성에 대한 차이는 가스 함유량, 온도, 점도의 차이와 직접적으로 관련된다.

② 유색 마그마는 그들 특성이 좀 더 유동체처럼 움직이기 때문에 규장질 마그마보다 더 격렬하다.

② 유색 화산은 하와이 제도에서 가장 일반적이며, 유색 마그마에 의해 만들어진 가장 좋은 예이다.

Part 3 Plants and animals in Deserts

1. ⑩	2. ⑩	3. Ⓐ	4. ⑩	5. Ⓐ	6. ⑩	7. Ⓑ
8. Ⓑ	9. Ⓐ	10. Ⓒ	11. ⑩	12. ⑩	13. ⑩	14. Ⓐ, Ⓒ, ⑩

1 The ability to deal with extreme heat is indispensable for plants and animals that occupy the desert. Water is an essential element in plant and animal survival in the desert due to the aridity of the habitat. All organisms require an **adequate** amount of water to survive. If the threshold is breached, organisms will die. Water is critical in ferrying nutrients throughout the plant and in serving as the foremost raw material in the photosynthetic process. A plant's ability to expand its body structure depends on the availability of water, soil texture, topographical distributions, and the proximity of large bodies of water. These elements account for why some areas cannot support any plant life and others have dense areas of plant growth. For this reason, rainforests have up to 100 times more plant life than in deserts in the same amount of land.

1 극심한 열을 다룰 수 있는 능력은 사막에 사는 식물과 동물에게 필수적이다. 물은 서식지의 건조함 때문에 사막에 사는 동식물에게 필수 요소이다. 모든 생물들은 생존하기 위해 적당한 양의 물이 필요하다. 만약 한계점을 넘게 된다면, 생물들은 죽을 것이다. 물은 영양소를 식물 곳곳에 운반하고 광합성 과정에서 가장 중요한 원료를 제공하는 역할을 한다. 식물의 몸체 구조를 확장시키는 능력은 물의 이용 가능성, 토성, 지형적인 분포, 그리고 많은 물줄기들과의 접근성에 달려 있다. 이러한 요소들이 왜 몇몇 지역은 어떤 식물도 살지 못하게 하고, 다른 지역은 식물 성장의 밀접한 지역을 이루는지 설명해 준다. 이러한 이유로, 같은 양의 땅에서도 열대우림은 사막보다 100배나 더 많은 식물을 가지고 있다.

2 Most plants of the desert fall into two main categories. The first is short-living ephemerals. The second is long-living perennials. The entire desert plants are under the above mentioned categories. When a certain level of rainfall is available, ephemerals absorb the water rapidly and grow vigorously, producing large quantities of fruits and flowers due to their short life cycles. However, immediate death ensues when there is not an adequate amount of water to sustain its growth as plants do not have any organic mechanisms to retain fluids. Fortunately, these plants successfully finish their cycle and plant their seeds before this occurs. These seeds lay dormant under the soil throughout the period of drought, and grow once the weather is favorable and wet. The long-living perennials have developed several different survival mechanisms to

2 사막에 사는 대부분의 식물들은 두 가지 주요 종류로 나뉜다. 첫 번째는 짧게 사는 단명 식물이다. 두 번째는 오래 사는 다년생 식물이다. 모든 사막의 식물들은 위에서 언급한 종류에 속한다. 어느 정도의 강우량이 사용 가능할 때, 단명 식물은 빠르게 물을 흡수하고 그들의 짧은 생명 주기 때문에 많은 양의 열매와 꽃들을 생산하면서 활발하게 자란다. 그러나 식물들이 수분을 보유할 어떤 유기적인 방법도 가지고 있지 않아서 성장을 지탱할 적당한 양의 물이 없을 때 즉각적인 죽음이 뒤따른다. 다행스럽게도, 이러한 식물들은 그들의 순환을 성공적으로 마치고 죽기 전에 씨앗을 심는다. 이러한 씨앗들은 가뭄 기간 동안 땅 아래에서 휴면기를 가지고 있다가 날씨가 좋고 습기가 있을 때

withstand dry seasons. Most of these perennials grow extremely dense hairs to cover waxy leaves to prevent water loss through evaporation while others limit their growth to low heights and wide widths to lay down extensive root systems. That people can see many of these plants which have root systems that easily stretch beyond ten meters underground in all directions is not unfamiliar. Succulents are able to keep water within their systems in times of desperate need as seen in cacti. Other plants have evolved a type of hard woody shell to prevent an external collapse due to the lack of water in its interior. Phreatophytes are another type of perennial that grows extremely long roots in search of a guaranteed pool of underground water. Some examples include date trees and tamarinds.

3 Animals are not so stationary like plants that they have developed behavioral instincts to survive in extreme temperature of the deserts. Most animals either retreat or escape the heat. Aestivation is one method of escaping the heat by going under a state of torpidity or dormancy in a friendly environment such as in a shaded cave. This survival tactic is mostly seen in reptiles and amphibians of the desert as the animal is able to almost stop all of its bodily processes and decrease overall temperature. Dormancy of this manner requires fewer nutrients to survive and is required in overcoming droughts. It is not until favorable conditions that the animals can return to a normal state. However, it is a quite 'light' state of dormancy. A study done on snails which are native to parts of Europe and Northern Africa shows that they can wake from their dormant state within ten minutes of being introduced to a wetter environment. The migration of animals in different seasons is another method of defeating the desert heat. Birds

성장한다. 오래 사는 다년생 식물들은 건기를 견뎌낼 수 있는 몇몇 다른 생존 방법을 개발시켜왔다. 대부분의 이러한 다년생 식물들은 증발을 통한 물의 손실을 막기 위해 광이 나는 잎들을 덮는 극도로 빽빽한 털이 자라고, 반면 다른 것들은 넓은 뿌리 체계를 내리기 위해 그들의 성장을 낮은 높이와 넓은 너비로 제한한다. 사람들이 10미터 너머의 땅에서 모든 방향으로 쉽게 뻗는 뿌리 체계를 가진 이러한 식물들 중 많은 것들을 볼 수 있는 것은 낯선 것이 아니다. 다육식물은 선인장류에서 볼 수 있듯이 극도로 물이 필요할 때 그들의 몸에 물을 보관할 수 있다. 다른 식물들은 체내에 물이 부족하기 때문에 외부의 붕괴를 막기 위해 단단한 목질의 껍질의 유형으로 진화했다. 심근식물들은 확실한 지하수의 웅덩이를 찾아서 극도로 긴 뿌리가 자라는 다년생 식물의 또 다른 종류이다. 몇몇 실례들은 종려나무와 타마린드를 포함한다.

3 동물들은 식물들처럼 그렇게 고정된 것이 아니므로 사막의 극심한 온도에서 살아남기 위해 행동 본능을 발달시켜왔다. 대부분의 동물들은 열에서 도피하거나 벗어난다. 여름잠은 그늘이 있는 동굴과 같은 친숙한 환경에서 휴면이나 휴지의 상태로 지내는 것으로 열을 피하는 방법들 중 하나이다. 이 생존 전략은 그 동물이 모든 몸의 과정을 멈추고 전체적인 온도를 낮출 수 있는 파충류나 양서류에서 대부분 발견된다. 이런 방식의 휴면은 살기 위해서 보다 적은 영양소를 필요로 하며, 가뭄을 극복하기 위해 필요하다. 그것은 동물들이 정상적인 상태로 돌아올 수 있는 유리한 조건들이 있어야 비로소 가능하다. 그러나 이것은 꽤 가벼운 상태의 휴면이다. 유럽과 북아프리카가 원산지인 달팽이에 대해 행해진 한 연구는 그들이 더 습윤한 환경이 시작되고 10분 내로 그들의 휴면기로부터 깰 수 있는 것을 보여

and mammals are mainly responsible for this survival tactic. Some animals cannot endure the extreme heat, and they escape by migrating a handful of miles out of a valley and up into the mountains. Mule deer in the American southwest seasonally complete this cycle between mountain and desert, as do juncoes, white-crowned sparrows and goshawks. Ⓐ ■ The daily living cycle of animals involves retreat as it is only a temporary escape from the dry and heat. Ⓑ ■ For example, during the hottest hours of a particular day, birds will rest under the refuge of a shaded nest. Ⓒ ■ Mammals also use a similar method as seen in kangaroo rat that will dig its way underground during these times. Ⓓ ■

준다. 다른 계절에 동물들의 이동은 사막의 열기를 물리치는 또 다른 방법이다. 새들과 포유류들은 이러한 생존 전략을 주로 담당한다. 몇몇 동물들은 극도의 열기를 견딜 수 없고, 그들은 골짜기에서부터 적은 마일 이동하여 벗어나고 산으로 올라간다. 미국 남서쪽의 뮬사슴은 검은방울새, 노랑턱멧새 그리고 참매처럼 정기적으로 산과 사막 사이에서 이러한 순환을 마무리한다. 동물들의 일일 생명주기는 건조함과 열기로부터의 일시적인 탈출뿐인 도피를 포함한다. 예를 들어, 특정한 날에 가장 더운 시간들 동안, 새들은 피난처인 그늘진 둥지 아래서 쉰다. 포유류는 또한 이러한 시간 동안 길을 땅 아래에 파는 캥거루 쥐에게서 보이는 유사한 방법을 사용한다.

어휘_ indispensable 꼭 필수적인 breach 위반하다 occupy 차지하다 aridity 건조함 adequate 충분한 raw material 원자재 proximity 근접성 ephemeral 단명식물 perennial 다년생식물 vigorously 혈기왕성하게 dormant 휴지의 height 높이 evaporation 증발 retreat 후퇴하다 amphibian 양서류 reptile 파충류 overcome 극복하다 defeat 패배시키다

1. The word adequate in the passage is closest in
meaning to
   Ⓐ innovative
   Ⓑ certain
   Ⓒ crucial
   Ⓓ sufficient

지문의 단어 adequate와 의미가 가장 가까운
것은?
   Ⓐ 획기적인
   Ⓑ 확실한
   Ⓒ 중대한
   Ⓓ 충분한

2. According to paragraph 1, which of the following is
NOT the role of water in plant life that lives in desert
environments?
   Ⓐ It is crucial for photosynthetic processes.
   Ⓑ If a certain amount of water is not satisfied, the
   plant will die.
   Ⓒ Transporting nutrients is one of the roles in water.
   Ⓓ Soil texture is determined by plant's physical ability.

단락 1에 따르면, 다음 중 어떤 것이 사막 환경
에 사는 식물들에 대한 물의 역할이 아닌가?
   Ⓐ 그것은 광합성 과정에서 중요하다.
   Ⓑ 만약 일정량의 물이 충족되지 못하면, 식물
   은 죽을 것이다.
   Ⓒ 영양소의 운반은 물의 역할 중 하나이다.
   Ⓓ 토양의 질감은 식물의 물리적 기능에서 필
   수적인 요소이다.

3. What can be inferred about ephemerals in paragraph
2?
   Ⓐ They need water to survive in the desert.
   Ⓑ They photosynthesize at a fast rate at any location.
   Ⓒ They need more water to survive in environment
   than do perennials.
   Ⓓ They take a long time to grow.

단락 2에서 단명식물에 대해 추측할 수 있는 것은?
   Ⓐ 그들은 사막에서 생존하기 위해 물이 필요
   하다.
   Ⓑ 그들은 어떤 장소에서든 빠른 속도로 광합
   성을 한다.
   Ⓒ 그들은 다년생 식물보다 환경에 더 취약하다.
   Ⓓ 그들은 자라는 데 시간이 오래 걸린다.

4. In what way is paragraph 2 presented?
   Ⓐ Types of plants are identified and the weaker type
   io fooused on.
   Ⓑ The author lists the names of plants.
   Ⓒ The author splits the plants into two groups and
   lists the flaws of each group.
   Ⓓ The author categorizes the plants into two groups
   and explains the characteristic of the plants.

단락 2에서는 어떤 방식을 제시하는가?
   Ⓐ 식물의 종류들을 확인하고 더 약한 종류에
   초점을 맞춘다.
   Ⓑ 작가가 식물의 이름을 열거한다.
   Ⓒ 작가가 식물들을 두 그룹으로 나누고 각
   그룹의 단점을 열거한다.
   Ⓓ 작가가 식물들을 두 그룹으로 분류하고 식
   물들의 성격을 설명한다.

5. The word withstand in the passage is closest in meaning to
   Ⓐ endure
   Ⓑ assemble
   Ⓒ follow
   Ⓓ resemble

지문의 단어 withstand와 의미가 가장 가까운 것은?
   Ⓐ 견디다
   Ⓑ 모으다
   Ⓒ 뒤를 잇다
   Ⓓ 유사하다

6. Which of the following is NOT mentioned about perennial adaptation?
   Ⓐ They have dense hair to cover leaves on their plants.
   Ⓑ They control their body size.
   Ⓒ They have extensive root system.
   Ⓓ They hide in their environments.

다음 중 다년생 식물의 적응에 대해 언급되지 않은 것은?
   Ⓐ 그들은 식물의 잎을 덮기 위해 빽빽한 털을 가지고 있다.
   Ⓑ 그들은 그들의 본체 크기를 조절한다.
   Ⓒ 그들은 넓은 뿌리 체계를 가지고 있다.
   Ⓓ 그들은 그들의 환경에 숨는다.

7. Why does the author mention cacti in paragraph 2?
   Ⓐ To indicate that the plant can be seen in the extremely hot area
   Ⓑ To provide an example of plants that shows how plants deal with the deficiency of water when water is desperate
   Ⓒ To represent that cacti develop external coating to prevent water ventilation
   Ⓓ To give an example of the plant having extension of roots

작가가 단락 2에서 cacti를 언급한 이유는?
   Ⓐ 그 식물을 극도로 더운 지역에서 볼 수 있다는 것을 나타내기 위해서
   Ⓑ 물이 절박할 때 어떻게 식물이 물의 결핍을 다루는지 보여주는 식물의 예시를 제공하기 위해서
   Ⓒ 선인장류가 물 환기의 방지를 위해 외부 코팅을 발달시키는 것을 보여주기 위해서
   Ⓓ 뿌리의 확대를 가진 식물의 예를 주기 위해서

8. The word stationary in the passage is closest in meaning to
   Ⓐ wandering
   Ⓑ immobile
   Ⓒ primitive
   Ⓓ secured

지문의 단어 stationary와 의미가 가장 가까운 것은?
   Ⓐ 방랑하는
   Ⓑ 움직이지 않는
   Ⓒ 초기의
   Ⓓ 보증된

9. According to paragraph 3, which of the following best explains the term aestivation?

Ⓐ It is a decrease in physiological processes in an area away from the heat.

Ⓑ It is the more favorable adaptation than other tactics.

Ⓒ An animal is no longer able to facilitate normal functioning.

Ⓓ An animal becomes dormant for a certain period every year.

단락 3에 따르면, 다음 중 어떤 것이 여름잠이라는 용어를 가장 잘 설명하는가?

Ⓐ 그것은 열기로부터 떨어진 곳에서의 생리적 과정의 감소이다.

Ⓑ 그것은 다른 전략보다 더 유리한 적응이다.

Ⓒ 동물이 더 이상 정상적인 기능이 가능하지 않다.

Ⓓ 동물이 매년 특정한 시기에 휴면하게 된다.

10. Which of the sentences below best expresses the most important information in the highlighted section of the passage? *Incorrect answer choices change the meaning in important ways or leave out essential information.*

Ⓐ A shaded cave provides animals with high level of adaptability of dormancy.

Ⓑ Dormancy is an adaptation which enables animals to adapt to their pleasant habitats such as in a shaded cave.

Ⓒ Aestivation helps animals escape from heat with minimized metabolic rates in hospitable setting.

Ⓓ Whether animals can endure certain amount of heat or not has little to do with their survival in the friendly environment.

아래의 문장 중 하이라이트된 지문의 가장 중요한 정보를 가장 잘 표현한 것은 무엇인가? 오답을 선택하면 중요한 면에서 의미를 왜곡하거나 필수적인 정보를 누락시키게 된다.

Ⓐ 그늘진 동굴이 동물들에게 휴면기의 높은 수준의 적응력을 제공한다.

Ⓑ 휴면기는 동물들이 그늘진 동굴 속과 같은 쾌적한 서식지에서 적응하는 것을 가능하게 하는 적응이다.

Ⓒ 여름잠은 쾌적한 환경에서 대사율을 최소화하여 동물들이 열기로부터 벗어날 수 있게 도와준다.

Ⓓ 동물들이 일정량의 열기를 견딜 수 있는지 아닌지는 친숙한 환경에서의 그들의 생존과 거의 관련이 없다.

11. The word they in the passage refers to

Ⓐ birds

Ⓑ mammals

Ⓒ snails

Ⓓ animals

지문에서 they가 의미하는 것은?

Ⓐ 새들

Ⓑ 포유류들

Ⓒ 달팽이들

Ⓓ 동물들

12. According to the paragraph 4, which animal has different type of adaptation from others?

Ⓐ Mule deer

Ⓑ Mammals

Ⓒ Sparrows

Ⓓ Snails

단락 4에 따르면, 다음 중 어떤 동물이 다른 동물들과 다른 종류의 적응력을 갖는가?

Ⓐ 물사슴

Ⓑ 포유류

Ⓒ 참새

Ⓓ 달팽이

13. Look at the four squares [■] that indicate where the following sentence can be added to the passage.

Advantages of such burrows include the coolness of the earth.

Where would the sentence best fit?

14. **Directions:** An introduction for a short summary of the passage appears below. Complete the summary by selecting the **THREE** answer choices that mention the most important points in the passage. Some sentences do not belong in the summary because they express ideas that are not presented in the passage or are minor ideas in the passage. **This question is worth 2 point.**

In plants that are found in desert environments, water is essential in a variety of different aspects that affect the amount of their growth and area of their distribution.

-
-
-

Ⓐ There are two families of desert plants and each group has disparate survival skills made toward living in drought situations.

Ⓑ Ephemerals quickly grow and die just as fast, planting seeds that do not emerge until a certain amount of water becomes available in the wet season.

Ⓒ Some of the evolutionary adaptations for plants that are able to live during the dry season involve finishing their reproductive cycle promptly and coatings on the plant, the ability to store water, and extremely large root structures that continuously search for water.

Ⓓ Animals can either escape the heat through aestivation, or migration and retreat by staying in cool places during the hottest part of the day.

다음 문장이 지문의 어느 곳에 추가될 수 있는 지를 나타내는 네 개의 정사각형을 보시오.

그러한 굴들의 장점은 땅의 시원함을 포함한다.

이 문장이 어디에 가장 적절하겠는가?

지문의 짧은 요약을 위한 소개문이 아래에 나와 있다. 지문에서 가장 중요한 요점을 나타내는 정답 3개를 선택해서 요약문을 완성하시오. 몇 몇 문장은 지문에 제시되지 않거나 중요하지 않 은 생각을 표현하기 때문에 요약에 포함되지 않 았다. 이 문제는 2점이다.

사막 환경에서 발견되는 식물들에 있어서 물은 식물들의 성장의 양에 영향을 미치는 여러 가지 의 다른 측면들과 이것의 분포 지역에서 필수적 이다.

-
-
-

Ⓐ 사막 식물에는 2개의 과(科)가 있고, 각각 의 그룹은 건조한 환경에서 살 수 있도록 만들어 주는 이질적인 생존 기술을 가지고 있다.

Ⓑ 단명 식물은 빠르게 자라고 빠르게 죽으며, 식물 종자는 우기에 특정한 양의 물이 이 용 가능하기 전에 나타나지 않는다.

Ⓒ 건기 동안 살 수 있도록 해 주는 식물들의 몇몇 진화적인 적응은 그들의 생식 주기를 빠르게 끝마치고, 물을 저장하는 능력인 식 물의 막과 계속해서 물을 찾는 굉장히 큰 뿌리 구조를 포함한다.

Ⓓ 동물들은 하루의 가장 더운 시간 동안 여 름잠이나 시원한 장소에서 지내면서 이동 하거나 도피하는 것을 통해 열기를 피한다.

Ⓔ While mammals choose to dig into the ground to retreat from the heat, reptiles and amphibians are physically adapted to deserts as they are able to go into a state of dormancy.

Ⓕ Behavioral or physical adaptions are present in all animals in order for them to find survival and success in deserts.

Ⓔ 포유류가 열기로부터 도피하기 위해 땅 속으로 굴을 파는 것을 선택하는 반면, 파충류나 양서류는 휴면기 상태로 들어가는 것처럼 사막에 신체적으로 적응되었다.

Ⓕ 행동의 혹은 신체적인 적응은 동물들이 사막에서의 생존과 성공을 찾기 위해서 모든 동물에게서 나타난다.

Part 1   Questions 1-5

Test3_Listening_Part1_01-05.mp3

| 1. ⓒ | 2. Ⓑ | 3. Ⓑ | 4. Ⓐ | 5. Ⓐ |

정답 및 해설

[Questions 1-5] Listen to part of a conversation between a student and staff member.

M(student) Hello, is this the administrative office?
W(staff) Yes, that's right.

M Great. Um, I'm here because of my school club. We were wondering if we could apply for an office on campus?
W Oh. Hmm. Well, we're out of private offices. How about a semi-private option? I can offer you a larger work space but you'll have to share with two other clubs. Each club gets a separate work area, but you'll all be sharing the same room.

M Huh. Will there be divider walls? You know, for some privacy?
W Yes, of course.

M Okay, I'll take it. Everyone in the club is really hyped up about getting an office.
W It is an exciting step. Okay, you need to fill out these two forms. But first, I need to ask you some questions so I can enter your application into the computer system.

M Sure, ask away.
W Your club name? And the president's last name?

M It's the photography club. And the president is John Williams. Williams, that's me.

M 안녕하세요, 여기 학교 행정실인가요?
W 네, 맞습니다.

M 아 그렇군요. 학교 클럽 문의 때문에 왔는데요. 혹시 학교 캠퍼스에 클럽 사무실을 신청할 수 있을까 해서요
W 음... 클럽 전용 사무실은 남은 게 없습니다. 혹시 준전용 사무실은 어떠세요? 제가 넓은 사무실은 제공할 수 있어요. 하지만 다른 두 개의 클럽은 공간을 함께 써야 해요. 클럽은 각각의 독립된 업무(사무) 공간을 가지는 대신 같은 사무실을 공유하게 돼요.

M 아. 거기 칸막이 벽(파티션)이 있나요? 사실 전용 공간이 좀 필요하거든요.
W 네 물론이죠.

M 좋아요. 그 사무실로 할게요. 모든 클럽 사람들이 사무실 얻는 것에 들떠 있거든요.
W 신나겠는데요. 좋아요. 여기 두 개의 양식을 작성해야 해요. 그러나 먼저 당신의 신청서를 컴퓨터 시스템에 입력하는 데 필요한 몇 가지 질문이 있어요.

M 물론이죠. 물어보세요.
W 클럽 이름이 무엇이죠? 그리고 클럽회장의 이름이?

M 사진클럽이에요. 회장은 존 윌리엄스인데, 바로 저예요.

W Oh, so you're the president. Just wait a second… That's strange. Nothing is coming up on my screen. Who's your faculty advisor?

M Professor Sara Baker from the arts department.

W Still nothing. Your club doesn't seem to be in my records. I hope you don't mind, but is your club an established club?

M Ah, no. It's quite new, actually.

W Uh-huh. And did you complete the registration process?

M I did, last week. It was the first thing I did as president.

W That's good, since a club has to be registered before I can do anything. But right now, I don't see a record of registration. I don't think I can help you without it.

M But I thought everything was finalized last week.

W Do you have the registration approval letter with you?

M I do have one, but it's not with me at the moment. It's in my dorm room. Maybe I can come back later, with the letter and the other forms?

W That would be fine. By the way, are you familiar with the benefits of being a registered club?

M I did hear some. Let's see… The university permits us to set up a website, right? I'm looking forward to it, because I want to encourage my club members to share their ideas. It'll be like a photography blog.

W And there's more. You can borrow audio and visual equipment for free. Also, you get a club mailbox and a club email address. You can even post fliers and posters around campus,

---

W 오, 당신이 회장이군요. 잠시만요… 이상한데요. 컴퓨터 화면에 아무것도 뜨질 않아요. 담당 교수가 누구인가요?

M 예술학부의 사라 베이커 교수님인데요.

W 여전히 아무것도 안 뜨네요. 당신 클럽에 대한 기록이 없는 것 같아요. 괜찮으시다면, 혹시 등록된 클럽인가요?

M 아. 아니요. 사실 신규 클럽입니다.

W 아하. 클럽 등록 절차를 완료했나요?

M 지난주에 했어요. 클럽 회장으로서 처음 한 일인걸요.

W 좋아요. 제가 도와드리기 전에 클럽은 등록되어 있어야 해요. 그러나 지금은 제가 클럽 등록 정보를 확인할 수 없어요. 등록 정보 없이는 당신을 도와드릴 수 없습니다.

M 하지만 저는 지난주에 다 끝난 걸로 알고 있었어요.

W 등록 승인 문서를 가지고 있나요?

M 네. 그러나 지금은 저에게 없어요. 문서는 제 기숙사 방에 있어요. 혹시 나중에 다시 올 때 등록 문서와 함께 다른 양식도 가져와야 하나요?

W 그거면 돼요. 그런데 등록된 클럽이 갖는 혜택에 대해 알고 있나요?

M 조금 들었어요. 학교에서 클럽 웹 사이트를 구축을 승인해주죠. 맞죠? 정말 기대하고 있어요. 왜냐면 모든 클럽 멤버들이 서로의 아이디어를 공유하는 것을 장려하고 있거든요. 마치 사진 블로그처럼요.

W 거기에 더 있어요. 시청각 장비를 무료로 대여할 수 있고, 클럽 우편함과 클럽 이메일 주소를 얻을 수 있어요. 심지어 사람들에게 당신 클럽을 알리기 위한 전단지와 포스터를 학교 주변에 게시할 수 있죠. 그리고 아마 제일

to let people to know about your club. And perhaps most importantly, you can apply for funding to organize club events.

M That last part does sound good. I'm thinking about hiring professional speakers to come to our campus. I want to prepare an opportunity for students to listen to some practical advice. But that'll definitely come at a cost, so funding would be a big help.

중요한 것은 클럽 행사를 위한 지원금을 신청할 수 있다는 거예요.

M 마지막 부분은 정말 좋네요. 학교에 전문가(연사)를 고용하려고 생각 중이었거든요. 학생들이 실용적인 조언을 들을 수 있도록 기회를 준비하고 싶어서요. 하지만 그건 분명 돈이 좀 들 테니까 지원금이 정말 큰 도움이 될 거 같네요.

어휘_ semi-private option 준전용 사무실 hyped up 들뜨다

1. What is the conversation mainly about?
   Ⓐ Inviting public speakers for a club event
   Ⓑ Signing up for an established club
   Ⓒ Managing a school activity
   Ⓓ Completing registration for a school club

대화는 주로 어떤 것에 관한 것인가?
   Ⓐ 클럽 행사를 위해 연사를 초대하는 것
   Ⓑ 설립된 클럽을 등록하는 것
   Ⓒ 학교 활동을 운영하는 것
   Ⓓ 학교 클럽의 등록을 완료하는 것

2. Why does the woman offer a semi-private office?
   Ⓐ Because only registered clubs can get private offices
   Ⓑ Because space is limited on campus
   Ⓒ Because the photography club has any few members
   Ⓓ Because the student cannot afford a private office

여자는 왜 준전용 사무실을 제안하는가?
   Ⓐ 오직 등록된 클럽만이 전용 사무실을 얻을 수 있기 때문에
   Ⓑ 학교 내 공간의 제한 때문에
   Ⓒ 사진 클럽 인원이 적기 때문에
   Ⓓ 학생이 전용 사무실을 사용할 형편이 안 되기 때문에

3. Why does the woman ask the name of the faculty advisor?
   Ⓐ Because she is planning to question the faculty advisor about the club
   Ⓑ Because she is trying to check the status of the club on her computer
   Ⓒ Because she is confirming that the club has an official supervisor
   Ⓓ Because she has no idea how to help the student

여자는 왜 담당 교직원의 이름을 물어보는가?
   Ⓐ 그녀는 클럽에 대해 담당 교직원에게 질문하려고 하기 때문에
   Ⓑ 그녀는 컴퓨터 시스템에서 클럽의 조건을 확인하려고 하기 때문에
   Ⓒ 그녀는 클럽이 공식적인 관리자가 있는지를 확인하려고 하기 때문에
   Ⓓ 그녀는 학생을 어떻게 도울지 모르기 때문에

Your club doesn't seem to be in my records. I hope you don't mind, but is your club an established club?

당신 클럽에 대한 기록이 없는 것 같아요. 괜찮으시다면, 혹시 등록된 클럽인가요?

4. Why does the woman say this: 🎧 "I hope you don't mind,"
   Ⓐ To attempt to help the student in a polite fashion
   Ⓑ To express doubt about the establishment of the club
   Ⓒ To suggest that there are too many photography clubs
   Ⓓ To make conversation while searching for the records

여자가 다음과 같이 말한 이유는? "괜찮으시다면,"
   Ⓐ 학생에게 정중한 방식으로 도움을 주기를 위해
   Ⓑ 클럽의 설립에 대해 의심을 표현하기 위해
   Ⓒ 너무 많은 사진 클럽들이 있다는 것을 제안하기 위해
   Ⓓ 정보를 찾는 동안 대화를 하기 위해

5. What will the student probably do following the conversation?
   Ⓐ Return to his dormitory room
   Ⓑ Register his club officially
   Ⓒ Check the office he has been given
   Ⓓ Gather members for his club

대화 이후에 학생은 무엇을 할 것인가?
   Ⓐ 기숙사로 돌아간다.
   Ⓑ 공식적으로 클럽을 등록한다.
   Ⓒ 주어진 사무실을 확인한다.
   Ⓓ 클럽 멤버들을 모집한다.

6. Ⓓ **7.** Ⓒ **8.** Ⓐ **9.** Ⓓ

10. Promote - Neither - Demote - Promote **11.** Ⓑ

[Questions 6-11] Listen to part of a lecture in an architecture class.

P In today's class, we will discuss the relationship between architectural design and sound mechanisms. For example, certain theaters or concert halls are designed to promote the delivery of sound. Now, what would be the most essential aspect of such architectural designs?
S Acoustics?

P Right! The study of accoustics, the sound delivery mechanism of auditoriums, has been researched and developed for over 2,000 years. However, the study of accoustics only became an officially recognized field of science at the beginning of the twentieth century. This is also the time when Wallace Sabine came up with his study of reverberation.

Well, Sabine tried to examine the reason why the students could not hear the lectures from professors very well at the Boston Lecture Hall. In order to figure this out, he formulated a series of experiments using the reverberation technique. Now, what does reverberation mean? It is a measure of sound persistency after the speaker or the source of the sound ceases to produce that sound. Reverberant sound is created when a sound wave hits the ceilings, walls, or floors of the architecture and echoes back the sound to a different location of the room. Of course, due to this effect, the acoustic properties of the room interior will play a huge part in the duration of the reverberation. Recognizing this phenomenon, Sabine formulated a mathematical equation to figure out a particular architecture's reverberation capacity. Now, the question is what will happen if the reverberation time is extended greatly?

P 오늘 강의에서, 우리는 건축 디자인과 소리 원리의 관계에 대해 논의하겠습니다. 예를 들어, 특정 무대나 콘서트 홀은 소리 전달을 촉진시키기 위해 만들어졌습니다. 그럼, 그러한 건축 디자인의 가장 중요한 측면으로는 무엇이 있을까요?
S 음향학인가요?

P 맞아요. 여러분도 알다시피 음향학의 연구, 즉 강당의 소리 전달 원리는 2,000년 이상 연구되고 개발되었습니다. 그러나, 음향학의 연구는 20세기 초에 공식적으로 과학의 분야로 인정되었습니다. 이것은 또한 Wallace Sabine이 (소리의) 반향의 연구를 시작한 시기이기도 합니다.

음, Sabine은 보스턴 강의실에서 학생들이 교수의 강의를 제대로 들을 수 없는 이유를 찾으려고 시도했습니다. 이유를 알아내기 위해, 그는 반향 기술을 사용하는 다양한 실험을 계획했습니다. 그럼, 반향이라는 것이 무엇을 의미하나요? 이것은 화자나 소리의 원천이 소리 내는 것을 멈춘 후에 소리의 지속성을 측정하는 것입니다. 반향은 방의 다른 위치에서 소리가 돌아 울려 퍼지고, 건축물의 바닥과 벽과 천장에 부딪힐 때 만들어집니다. 당연히, 이 효과 때문에, 방 내부의 음향적인 특징은 반향의 지속에 큰 역할을 합니다. 이 효과를 인식하면서, Sabine은 특정 건축물의 반향 능력을 계산해 내는 수학 공식을 만들어 냈습니다. 그럼, 질문은, 만약 반향이 무척 오래 지속되면 무슨 일이 일어날까요?

S Wouldn't too much echoing make it even more difficult to hear the sound clearly and easily?

P Yes! As you said, too much reverberation does not promote a clear and effective delivery of sound. However, when the reverberation duration is too short, the sound dies quickly. The speaker or performer would have a very hard time trying to get their message across. The room needs to be alive; it needs to be full with sound. This is why we have to manipulate reverberation using architectural designs. We wouldn't want to make things hard for the speakers or the performers, would we? In that case, what could be the important conditions that we must consider for designing an auditorium or a theater?

S I don't know. Size, maybe?

P Sure! A larger room size will certainly increase the duration of reverberation. One important factor to think about is the purpose of that particular room – whether it will be used for speech and lectures or for music and concerts. For example, a concert hall designed for orchestras need to be very large in order to deliver the sound of music effectively. Of course, there are certain exceptions; if the room is designed for small recitals like piano practices, the room would have to be a lot smaller.

S Along that line, I remember reading that the symphony orchestra concert halls are too large for jazz concerts because the hall carries too much echo.

P That's not surprising. Jazz is usually played in small groups, and would probably require a shorter reverberation for an effective sound delivery.

In addition to the size of the room, the shape and the texture of the room also play an important

S 너무 많은 소리의 울림은 소리를 분명하고 명확하게 듣기 더 어렵게 만들지 않을까요?

P 맞아요. 학생이 설명했듯이, 너무 많은 반향은 효과적이고 분명한 소리의 전달을 촉진시키지 못합니다. 하지만, 반향의 지속이 너무 짧으면 소리는 금방 사라집니다. 화자나 연기자가 메시지를 전달하는 데 어려움을 겪을 수 있죠. 방은 생동감이 있어야 합니다. 소리로 가득 찰 필요가 있지요. 이것이 우리가 건축적인 디자인을 이용하여 반향을 조정해야 하는 이유입니다. 우리가 화자나 연기자를 힘들게 하고 싶진 않잖아요. 그렇죠? 그러면, 강당이나 무대를 만들 때 고려해야만 하는 중요한 조건들이 무엇일까요?

S 잘 모르겠어요. 혹시, 크기인가요?

P 맞아요. 큰 방의 크기는 확실히 반향의 지속 시간을 증가시킵니다. 고려해야 할 한 가지 중요한 점은 특정 방의 목적입니다. – 강연이나 연설 또는 음악이나 콘서트 등 어떤 용도로 사용되든지 간에 말이죠. 예를 들어, 오케스트라를 위해 지어진 콘서트홀은 음악 소리를 효과적으로 전달하기 위해 매우 큰 공간이 필요합니다. 당연히 특정 예외들은 존재합니다. 예를 들어 방이 피아노 연습처럼 작은 리사이틀을 위해 만들어진다면, 훨씬 작아야만 합니다.

S 같은 맥락에서, 저는 오케스트라 심포니를 위한 콘서트홀은 너무 많은 울림을 만들기 때문에 재즈 콘서트에는 너무 크다는 것을 읽은 기억이 나네요.

P 그것은 놀라운 일이 아닙니다. 재즈는 대개 작은 그룹으로 연주되고, 아마도 효과적인 소리 전달을 위해 더 짧은 반향을 요구합니다.

방의 크기와 더불어 방의 모양과 질감도 반향에 영향을 주는 중요한 역할을 합니다. 이 내용을 다

role in affecting the reverberation. Let's think about this in a different way. Imagine that the sound wave is a squash ball and you are trying to hit this ball against the wall. Sure, it will bounce off and hit multiple walls and even the ceiling. Yet, a single strike against a perfectly parallel wall wouldn't bounce the ball back and it would be hard for the ball to hit all sides of the squash court. If the walls had wrinkles or pointy corners it would make the ball bounce around even more. This phenomenon teaches us that the architectural design must avoid straight and parallel walls or ceilings in order for the sound to be distributed evenly in all directions

S Is that really true? I think I've been to a concert hall with such parallel rectangular structures.

P I understand where you're coming from. The old concert halls that were built around the 19th century were mostly rectangular. Yet, if you think about it, there are a lot of decorations and ornaments near the wall that act as a medium to promote the distribution of sound within the room. Now, your question helped me remember another crucial variable that promotes sound delivery. The decorative items that are put in a room actually serve double duties; they are not merely set up to make the concert hall look nicer. For instance, the beautiful chandeliers that are hung on the ceiling of the hall very effectively diffuse sound. Furthermore, the plush chairs set up around the hall are very efficient absorbers of the sound, softening the reverberation level. They are all carefully calculated set ups that are used not only to decorate rooms but also to enhance the details of the sound and music played within the room.

른 방식으로 생각하자면, 음파를 스쿼시 공이라고 생각하고, 벽에 대고 공을 때린다고 생각해 봅시다. 당연히, 공은 튕겨져 나갈 것이고, 천장을 포함한 여러 개의 벽들을 칠 것입니다. 그러나 벽과 완벽하게 수평으로 한 번 친 공은 튕겨 오지 않을 것이고 공이 스쿼시 코트의 모든 면을 치기 힘들 것입니다. 만약 벽이 구부러져 있거나 뾰족한 부분이 있다면, 공은 더 많이 튕겨질 것입니다. 그럼, 이 현상은 소리를 모든 방향으로 균등하게 나누기 위해서 건축 디자인은 직선이나 병렬로 놓인 벽이나 천장을 없애야만 한다는 것을 알려줍니다.

S 정말인가요? 그러나 제가 생각하기에 그런 병렬의 사각형 구조로 놓여 있는 콘서트홀에 가 본 적이 있어요.

P 어디에서 그런 생각을 했는지 이해하겠어요. 19세기 무렵에 지어진 오래된 콘서트홀은 대부분 사각형입니다. 그러나 만약 생각해 본다면, 벽 근처에 많은 장식들이 있다는 사실을 알게 될 겁니다. 이것들은 공간 내에서 소리의 전달을 촉진시키기 위한 매개체 역할을 하죠. 그럼, 학생의 질문은 소리의 전달을 향상시키는 다른 중요한 요소들을 기억나게 해주었습니다. 방에 놓인 장식품들은 단순히 콘서트홀을 더 보기 좋게 해주려는 것이 아니라 다른 목적을 갖고 있었습니다. 예를 들어, 홀의 천장에 매달려 있는 아름다운 샹들리에는 소리를 매우 효율적으로 분산시켜 줍니다. 게다가 홀 주변에 놓인 벨벳같이 안락한 천으로 만든 의자들은 반향의 정도를 부드럽게 해주면서 매우 효율적인 흡수제 역할을 합니다. 이것들은 단순히 방을 꾸미려고 사용된 것이 아니라 방에서 연주되는 음악과 소리를 향상시키기 위해 주의 깊게 계산된 장치들입니다.

어휘_ auditorium 강당 acoustics 음향학 reverberation (소리의) 반향 persistency 지속성 diffuse 분산시키다 plush 벨벳 같은 안락한 천

6. What is the lecture mainly about?
  Ⓐ Various historical architectures designed for effective sound delivery
  Ⓑ Various architectural factors that increase the reverberation duration
  Ⓒ The concept of how the size of the room changes the reverberation time
  Ⓓ The factors that have an influence on the persistence of sound

강의는 주로 무엇에 관한 것인가?
  Ⓐ 효과적인 음향 분산을 위한 다양한 역사 건축물
  Ⓑ 반향의 지속(시간)을 증가시키는 다양한 건축학적 요소들
  Ⓒ 방의 크기가 반향 시간을 어떻게 변하게 하는지에 대한 개념
  Ⓓ 소리의 지속에 영향을 미치는 요소들

7. How did Sabine contribute to the study of reverberation and architectural acoustics?
  Ⓐ Sabine spent a great deal of effort and time getting reverberation and acoustics accepted as an important fied of architectural science.
  Ⓑ Sabine designed the Boston Lecture Hall, which applied his concept of reverberation to make the place promote an effective delivery of sound.
  Ⓒ Sabine formulated the mathematical equation for reverberation, which later played an important role in the designs of effective auditoriums.
  Ⓓ Sabine conceived and built an architectural design that enhanced reverberation, resulting in better acoustic quality.

Sabine은 잔향과 건축학적 음향학에 어떻게 기여했는가?
  Ⓐ Sabine은 반향과 음향학이 건축 과학의 중요한 분야로 인정받도록 많은 시간과 노력을 쏟았다.
  Ⓑ Sabine은 그의 반향의 개념에 부합하는 공간이 더 효과적인 소리를 전달하게 만드는 보스턴 강의실을 디자인했다.
  Ⓒ Sabine은 후에 효과적인 강당을 짓는 역할을 하는 반향을 유도하는 수학 공식을 도출해냈다.
  Ⓓ Sabine은 더 좋은 음질을 유발하는 향상된 반향을 일으키는 건축 디자인을 만들어냈다.

8. According to the lecture, which of the following acoustic problem could occur if the room is too large?
  Ⓐ The big size of the room will create excessive reverberation and too much echoing.
  Ⓑ The big size of the room will significantly decrease repetitive echoing, and thereby decrease the reverberation.
  Ⓒ The sound wave won't reach the walls of the big size rooms and won't reflect back and forth within the room.
  Ⓓ The sound wave will travel much more freely in the big size rooms, and will make too loud of a noise.

강의에 따르면, 방이 너무 크면 어떤 음향적 문제가 발생하는가?
  Ⓐ 방이 크면 과도한 반향과 몹시 큰 메아리가 발생할 것이다.
  Ⓑ 방이 크면 메아리 반복을 줄이고 그로 인해 반향을 감소시킬 것이다.
  Ⓒ 음파가 큰 방의 벽에 도달하지 못해서 방의 앞뒤로 전달되지 않을 것이다.
  Ⓓ 음파가 큰 방에서 더 자유롭게 움직여서 너무 시끄러운 소리를 낼 것이다.

9. Why does the professor mention squash?

Ⓐ To explain the rules of the sport that he enjoys playing

Ⓑ To suggest that if the squash court was bumpy instead of flat, the ball would more easily bounce in between the walls

Ⓒ To show that the reverberation will increase if the walls were parallel and straight

Ⓓ To analogically describe how sound travels and reflects against the walls

10. According to the lecture, which of the following architectural properties will promote or demote reverberation? If a property is not mentioned in the lecture or does not apply to either of choices, click on neither.

	Promote	Demote	Neither
Largely spaced rooms	○		
Oval shaped architectures			○
Flat and parallel walls		○	
Ceiling chandeliers	○		

교수는 왜 스쿼시를 언급하는가?

Ⓐ 그가 즐기는 스포츠의 규칙을 설명하기 위해서

Ⓑ 스쿼시 코트가 평평하지 않고 울퉁불퉁하다면 공이 벽들 사이에서 더 쉽게 튕겨져 나올 것이라고 제안하기 위해서

Ⓒ 벽이 수평이고 평평하다면 반향이 더 증가할 것이라는 것을 보여주기 위해서

Ⓓ 비유적으로 소리가 벽을 따라 튕겨지고 전달되는 것을 설명하기 위해서

강의에 따르면, 아래의 건축학적 요소 중 반향을 증가시키거나 감소시키는 요소는 무엇인가? 요소가 언급되지 않았거나 두 개의 선택에 적용되지 않으면 둘 다 아님에 체크하시오.

	증가	감소	둘 다 아님
크기가 큰 방	○		
원형 모양의 건축물			○
평평하고 평행의 벽		○	
벽에 걸린 샹들리에	○		

Listen again to a part of the conversation. Then answer the question.

강의의 일부분을 다시 듣고 물음에 답하시오.

P This is why we have to manipulate the reverberation using architectural designs. We wouldn't want to make things hard for the speakers or the performers, would we?

P 이것이 우리가 건축적인 디자인을 이용하여 반향을 조정해야 하는 이유입니다. 우리가 화자나 연기자를 힘들게 하고 싶진 않잖아요. 그렇죠?

11. What can be inferred when the professor says this: 🎧 "We wouldn't want to make things hard for the speakers or the performers, would we"?
Ⓐ It is hard to plan an architectural design that satisfies people of various artistic preferences
Ⓑ The quality of sound can have a great influence on a wide range of situations
Ⓒ It is a difficult task to create architecture that is expected to last for long periods of time
Ⓓ There are many speakers and musicians who are picky about architectural acoustics

아래 교수의 말에서 추론할 수 있는 사실은 무엇인가? "우리가 화자나 연기자를 힘들게 하고 싶진 않잖아요. 그렇죠?"
Ⓐ 다양한 예술적 선호도를 지닌 사람들을 만족시키는 건축 디자인을 만드는 것은 어렵다.
Ⓑ 소리의 질은 다양한 상황에 큰 영향을 미친다.
Ⓒ 오랜 시간 동안 지속되는 건축물을 만드는 것은 어렵다.
Ⓓ 건축학적 음향학에 까다로운 화자나 음악가가 많다.

Part 1 Questions 12-17

Test3_Listening_Part1_12-17.mp3

12. Ⓓ	13. Ⓓ	14. Ⓒ	15. Ⓓ	16. Ⓑ	17. Ⓒ

[Questions 12-17] Listen to part of a lecture in a psychology class.

Before I start today's lecture, I want to check if you have an idea of what psychology is. What is psychology? It's a cognitive science, focusing on mind and behavior – that is, cognition. And as you should remember, we started talking about animal cognition during our last lecture.

Okay, why do people want to study animal cognition? I mean, they're animal, not people, so why would it be relevant? Well, researchers want to figure out the relationship between animal and human cognition. They're curious about the analogy between how animals think and how

수업을 시작하기 전에, 심리학이 무엇인기에 대한 여러분의 생각을 알아보고 싶군요. 심리학이란 무엇인가요? 심리학은 정신과 행동에 중점을 두고 있는 인지과학입니다. 즉 인식이죠. 그리고 여러분이 기억하듯이, 우리는 지난 강의에서 동물 인지에 대해 이야기를 나눴습니다.

좋아요. 사람들은 왜 동물 인지에 대하여 공부하고자 할까요? 제 말뜻은, 그들이 사람이 아닌 동물이기 때문입니다. 그래서 왜 이것이 관련이 있을까요? 연구자들은 동물과 인간 인지 사이의 관련성을 파악하고자 합니다. 그들은 동물과 인간의 사고방식의 유사점에 대해 궁금해하죠. 그

people think. But since cognition encompasses many meanings, we'll just stick to metacognition. So what is metacognition? Well, simply put, it is being aware of one's thoughts or feelings. A person who knows what he or she knows or feels is a metacognitive being. So, we humans are all metacognitive individuals – but what about animals? When they make decisions, are they affected by their thoughts or feelings, like we are? That's what we want to find out.

To check for this capability in animals, we must conduct studies. Researchers found that two species of animals were well-suited for this experiment: dolphins and monkeys. They could be trained relatively easily compared to other animals and researchers expected that they could discern between certainty and uncertainty. These two are frequent subjects in psychological studies, even today. Anyway, the purpose of the experiment was to prove that animals can feel uncertain and make decisions based on their mental state.

First, let's talk about the study involving dolphins. The dolphins in this study were trained to recognize round blocks. A dolphin would have two paddles, and it was supposed to press the left paddle when it was shown a round block. If the block was square, then it had to press the right paddle. If it pressed the wrong paddle – say, if the block was round but it pressed the right paddle – then it resulted in a time-out. The experiment would stop for a few seconds and the dolphin would have to wait for a short period of time. Every time the dolphin pressed the right paddle, it received a food reward. After conducting the experiment several times, researchers noted that the dolphin acted differently during easy trials and difficult trials. If the trial was easy, the dolphin pressed the right paddle almost immediately. If the trial was hard, it took more time to decide – as if it were hesitating.

러나 인식은 많은 의미를 내포하기 때문에, 우리는 초인지(메타인지)에 대해서만 다루기로 합시다. 초인지란 무엇일까요? 간단하게 초인지란, 누군가의 생각이나 느낌을 알아차리는 것입니다. 본인이 의식하는 것 또는 느끼는 것을 알 수 있는 사람은 초인지적 존재입니다. 그래서 우리 각각의 인간은 모두 초인지적 존재겠죠. 그러나 동물의 경우는 어떨까요? 동물들이 결정을 내릴 때, 우리 인간처럼 그들의 생각이나 느낌(감정)이 영향을 미칠까요? 그것이 바로 우리가 알아보고자 하는 것입니다.

동물들의 이러한 능력을 확인할 수 있는 한 가지 방법은 연구를 수행하는 것입니다. 연구자들은 동물 두 종이 이 실험을 위해 잘 연구되었다는 것을 알아냈습니다. 돌고래와 원숭이죠. 이들은 다른 동물들과 비교해서 상대적으로 쉽게 훈련되고, 연구자들은 이들이 확실성과 불확실성 사이를 알아차릴 수 있다고 기대했습니다. 이 두 종은 오늘날까지도 심리연구에서 빈번한 연구주제입니다. 어쨌든, 실험의 목적은 동물들이 불확실(성)을 느끼고 그들의 정신 상태에 따라 결정을 내리는 것을 증명하는 것입니다.

첫째로, 돌고래와 관련된 연구에 대해서 이야기해 봅시다. 이 연구에서 돌고래는 원형 블록을 인식할 수 있게 훈련되었습니다. 돌고래에게 두 개의 패들이 주어지고, 원형 블록이 나타나면 왼쪽 패들을 누르게 됩니다. 만약 블록이 사각형이면, 오른쪽 패들을 누릅니다. 만약 잘못된 패들을 누르면, 예를 들어 만약 블록이 원형이었는데 오른쪽 패들을 누른 경우, 중간 휴식(Time-out)을 가지죠. 실험은 잠시 동안 멈추게 됩니다. 그리고 돌고래는 짧은 시간 대기하여야 합니다. 돌고래가 오른쪽 패들을 누른 모든 경우에는 음식이 제공됩니다. 몇 번의 실험을 한 후에, 연구자들은 쉬운 시도와 어려운 시도 동안 돌고래가 다르게 행동한 것에 대해 기록합니다. 만약 시도가 쉬웠다면, 돌고래는 거의 즉시 오른쪽 패들을 눌렀습니다. 시도가 어려웠다면, 결정하는 데 조금 더 많은 시간이 걸렸습니다. 마치 주저하는 것처럼 말이죠.

정답 및 해설

Next, a third option was introduced. The dolphin was given a third paddle that would begin a new trial. It was a "pass paddle" since it could be used to pass a difficult trial. When the dolphin figured this out, it often chose the third paddle during difficult trials. What do you think researchers took from this? They proposed that the uncertainty of the animal was reflected through its actions. However, other researchers criticized the conclusion, saying that it was a conditioned response. You should recall what a conditioned response is, as a learned response paired with a certain stimulus. They claimed that the dolphin was simply pressing the pass paddle to speed up the experiment and earn its food reward. In other words, the dolphin wasn't aware of feeling either certain or uncertain.

A more recent study following the dolphin study used monkeys. The monkeys were taught to identify light colors. You can see how it's analogous to the dolphin study, which required dolphins to identify blocks as round or square. Um, in the monkey study, trials were made difficult by showing colors of confusing hues. That is, the darker the color, the more difficult the trial. Oh, let's not forget the third option – the pass option. But the key difference of the monkey study was that four trials had to be finished before the monkeys received feedback. Until each experiment consisting of four trials was over, the test monkeys received no reward or punishment. In the experiment, monkeys chose the pass option during difficult trials, although the option wasn't associated with a reward. Thus, the study provided evidence against the claim that it was a conditioned response.

Today, we talked about cognitive processes of animals – are they aware of their feeling or state of mind? Well, we may never know, because we can't see inside their minds. What we can do, though, is to explore their metacognitive capacity.

다음으로, 세 번째 조건을 도입했습니다. 돌고래는 새로운 시도를 할 수 있는 제3의 패들을 가지게 되었죠. 바로 통과할 수 있는 패들이지요. 이것은 어려운 시도를 통과하는 데 사용되죠. 돌고래가 이것을 파악한 후에는 어려운 시험일 경우에 제3의 패들을 자주 골랐죠. 연구자들이 이것에서 무엇을 얻었다고 생각하세요? 그들은 동물의 불확실성이 그 행동에 반영된다고 제안했죠. 그러나 다른 연구자들은 그 결론을 조건 반응일 뿐이라며 비판했습니다. 여러분, 특정 자극에 동반되는, 학습된 반응으로서의 조건 반응이 무엇인가에 대해 상기해보세요. 그들은 돌고래가 실험을 빨리 해서 음식 보상을 받으려고 단순히 통과 패들을 누른다고 주장했습니다. 다시 말해, 돌고래는 확실한 느낌과 불확실한 느낌 중 어떤 것도 알아차리지 못한다는 것이죠.

돌고래 연구 다음의 최근 연구는 원숭이를 이용합니다. 원숭이는 엷은 색을 알아볼 수 있게 교육받았습니다. 여러분은 원형 또는 사각형 블록을 알아내는 돌고래 연구와 이것이 어떻게 유사한지 알아봐야 합니다. 음. 원숭이 연구에서는 혼동되는 색을 보여줌으로써 실험이 어렵게 구성됩니다. 즉 더 어두운 색일수록 실험은 더 어려워지는 거죠. 오, 제3의 조건인 통과 조건을 잊지 마세요. 그러나 원숭이 연구의 차별점은 원숭이가 피드백을 받기 전에 4번의 시도(실험)가 끝나야 한다는 것입니다. 4차례로 이루어져 있는 각 시도가 끝나기 전에, 실험 원숭이는 어떤 보상이나 벌을 받을 수 없습니다. 비록 그 옵션이 보상과 연관되지 않아도 원숭이는 어려운 실험일 때 통과 조건을 골랐습니다. 그러므로 이 연구는 조건 반응이라는 주장에 반하는 증거를 제공해주는 것이죠.

오늘날, 우리는 동물의 인지 과정에 대해 이야기했습니다. 동물들은 그들의 감정이나 정신 상태를 알 수 있을까요? 아마 우리는 이 사실을 절대로 알 수 없을 겁니다. 왜냐하면 우리는 그들의 마음속을 들여다볼 수 없으니까요. 우리가 할 수

By doing so, we can attempt to discover how our minds are similar or different from theirs.

있는 것이라곤 그들의 초인지 능력을 탐구하는 것입니다. 그렇게 함으로써 우리는 우리의 생각 (정신)이 어떻게 그들의 것과 유사한지 또는 차이가 있는지에 대해 찾으려고 시도할 수 있습니다.

어휘_ cognition 인식, 인지 analogy 유사점 encompass 포함하다 metacognitive 초인지 paddle 패들 stimulus 자극

정답 및 해설

12. What does the professor primarily discuss?
    ⓐ The reason why researchers are interested in animal psychology
    ⓑ The extent of research on the intelligence of dolphins and monkeys
    ⓒ The disadvantages of food rewards in studies involving animals
    ⓓ The studies concerning animals' awareness of feeling uncertainty

교수가 주로 논의하는 것은 무엇인가?
    ⓐ 연구자들이 동물 심리학에 흥미를 갖는 이유
    ⓑ 돌고래와 원숭이의 지능에 대한 연구의 확장
    ⓒ 동물이 관여한 연구들에서 음식 보상에 대한 단점들
    ⓓ 동물의 불확실성 감정 인지에 관한 연구들

13. Why do researchers study animal cognition?
    ⓐ To analyze the feelings and mental states that animals can experience
    ⓑ To prove that some species of animals exhibit high levels of intelligence
    ⓒ To understand mental capabilities of animals compared to those of humans
    ⓓ To investigate the thought pattern behind animals and humans make

연구자들은 왜 동물 인지를 실험하는가?
    ⓐ 동물이 경험할 수 있는 느낌과 정신 상태를 분석하기 위해서
    ⓑ 어떤 종의 동물들이 높은 지적 능력을 보이는지를 증명하기 위해서
    ⓒ 인간과 비교하여 동물의 정신 능력을 이해하기 위해서
    ⓓ 동물과 인간이 결정을 내릴 때 영향을 주는 요인을 조사하기 위해서

14. According to the professor, why are dolphins and monkeys utilized for psychological research?
    ⓐ They perform well on intelligence tests.
    ⓑ They have developed brains similar to those of humans.
    ⓒ They can be disciplined to carry out specific actions.
    ⓓ They understand human speech and communication.

교수에 따르면, 돌고래와 원숭이가 왜 심리학 연구에 이용되는가?
    ⓐ 그들은 지적 실험을 잘 수행한다.
    ⓑ 그들은 인간의 뇌와 유사하게 발달되어 있다.
    ⓒ 그들은 특정 행동을 수행하도록 훈련될 수 있다.
    ⓓ 그들은 인간의 대화를 이해할 수 있다.

15. What was the purpose of the pass paddle in the dolphin study?

   Ⓐ It was the correct option for blocks that were neither round nor square.

   Ⓑ It increased the probability that the dolphins would make the right choice.

   Ⓒ It showed the difficulty of the experiment.

   Ⓓ It attempted to demonstrate that dolphins could feel unsure.

돌고래 연구에서 패스 패들의 목적은 무엇인가?

   Ⓐ 패스 패들은 둥글지도 않고 사각형도 아닌 블록의 정답 선택이었다.

   Ⓑ 패스 패들은 돌고래가 올바른 정답을 맞히는 가능성을 높여줬다.

   Ⓒ 패스 패들은 실험의 어려움을 보여줬다.

   Ⓓ 패스 패들은 돌고래가 불확실함을 느낀다는 것을 증명하려는 시도였다.

16. Why did some researchers disagree with the conclusion of the dolphin study?

   Ⓐ Mental capacities of dolphins cannot be compared to those of humans.

   Ⓑ Responses could result from learned association rather than cognition.

   Ⓒ Options were unnecessarily numerous and confusing for the dolphins.

   Ⓓ Dolphins only chose the third option to avoid punishment.

몇몇 연구자들은 왜 돌고래 연구의 결과에 반대하였는가?

   Ⓐ 돌고래의 지적 능력은 인간과 비교될 수 없기 때문이다.

   Ⓑ 반응은 지적 능력보다는 학습과 연관된 결과이기 때문이다.

   Ⓒ 선택이 불필요하게 많았고 돌고래를 헷갈리게 했기 때문이다.

   Ⓓ 돌고래들은 처벌을 피하기 위해서만 제3의 조건을 선택했다.

17. Why did each experiment in the monkey study consist of four trials?

   Ⓐ To increase the accuracy of the experiment by conducting multiple trials

   Ⓑ To lengthen the time required for the completion of the experiment

   Ⓒ To prevent the monkeys from taking advantage of the pass option

   Ⓓ To raise the difficulty of the experiment by showing several colors

각각의 원숭이 실험은 왜 네 번의 시도로 이루어졌는가?

   Ⓐ 여러 번의 시도를 통해 실험의 정확성을 높이기 위해서

   Ⓑ 실험을 끝내는 시간을 측정하기 위해서

   Ⓒ 원숭이가 패스 선택을 이용하는 것을 막기 위해서

   Ⓓ 여러 색을 보여줌으로써 실험의 난이도를 높이기 위해서

1. Ⓑ   2. Ⓑ   3. Ⓒ   4. Ⓓ   5. Ⓐ

Listening

정답 및 해설

[Questions 1-5] Listen to part of a conversation between a student and a clerk.

S(Male) Hello, I'm looking for a book titled New Kind of Science written by Stephen Wolfram.

C(Female) Would you like me to help you find it?

S Well, I couldn't find it on the shelves.

C Hold on for a minute I'll check it on the computer. The author was?

S Stephen Wolfram

C Let's see… Well, this is strange; it is not on the registry. Are you sure this book is a course offered by our university?

S Yeah. The book is the officially assigned reading for my class curriculum.

C You are currently taking this class right? It's not like you are trying to buy the book in advance for the next semester or anything?

S No, I am currently enrolled in this semester's class.

C Is that so? I don't know why it's not coming up then.

S You know, actually, this is a course offered by the graduate school. Perhaps that could be why. I mean, I'm not grad student. I'm just taking a graduate level course as an undergrad student.

C I don't think that's the problem, grad or undergrad wouldn't make a difference. I guess there could have been a spelling error when the book's title was registered on our database, or maybe the book has been sold out. In a case the book is sold out, we can receive new shipments within a week.

S 안녕하세요. Stephen Wolfram이 쓴 「New Kind of Science」라는 책을 찾고 있어요.

C 책을 찾는 것을 도와드릴까요?

S 음, 책꽂이에서 책을 찾을 수가 없네요.

C 잠깐만요. 컴퓨터로 확인해 볼게요. 작가가…?

S Stephen Wolfram이요.

C 음, 그런데, 이상하네요. 등록되어 있는 게 없어요. 우리 대학에서 제공하는 과목이 확실한가요?

S 맞아요. 이 책은 수업 과정에 지정된 공식 과제 도서예요.

C 현재 이 수업을 듣는 거 맞죠? 다음 학기 책을 미리 사거나 하는 건 아니죠?

S 아니에요. 현재 이번 학기 수업에 등록된 상태예요.

C 그래요? 그럼 그 책이 왜 안 뜨는지 모르겠네요.

S 사실, 이 수업은 대학원에서 제공되는 수업이에요. 그래서 아마도 그럴 수도 있는데요. 제 말은 제가 대학원생이 아니에요. 대학생으로 그냥 대학원 과정의 수업을 듣는 거거든요.

C 그게 문제가 될 거 같진 않아요. 대학원생이나 대학생이나 큰 차이는 없어요. 제 추측으로는 데이터베이스에 책 제목을 등록할 때, 철자가 잘못 입력되어 있었을 수도 있을 것 같아요. 아니면 책이 다 팔렸을 수도 있고요. 만일에 책이 다 팔렸을 경우, 우리는 일주일 인에 새로운 배송을 받을 수 있어요.

S   I'm sorry, but I have to buy the book immediately. The professor already started assigning homework on the book. I guess I'll just have to check the library now.

C   Wait, let me check again if we've made any shipment orders for the book; the order information will also appear on our database. Let me see… Wolfram… Stephen… I'm sorry; I still don't see any records. It looks like we don't have the book as a part of our set.

S   Well, that's very strange.

C   Indeed. Can you give me the name of your professor? I can type up his name to search registered information about the course textbooks and see if it shows up on the computer. Let's see if that works things out.

S   It's Professor Kayne.

C   K, A, N, and E?

S   No, his spelling goes K, A and then Y, N, E. He is from the computer science department.

C   Is this a course offered by the computer science department?

S   Yup.

C   Now, I see the problem. I am aware that the computer bookstore across the street sells these computer science related books.

S   Really? Across the street? Why, I've never seen one. Did they put up any signs up nearby?

C   I'm not sure.

S   Wow, if they had put signs up and if I knew, I wouldn't have wasted my time and yours!

C   Well, anyhow, you'd better check out the computer bookstore across the street. I'm sure that they will have your book. If that's not the case, just return to me and I can assist you to look it up from other places. I can call

---

S   죄송해요, 하지만 저는 그 책을 지금 당장 사야만 해요. 교수님이 이미 책에서 과제를 내주셨거든요. 이제, 도서관에서 확인해 봐야겠네요.

C   잠깐만요. 제가 그 책을 주문한 게 있는지를 다시 확인해 볼게요. 주문 정보는 우리 데이터베이스에도 뜨거든요. 볼까요… Wolfram… Stephen… 죄송한데, 아무 기록도 발견할 수가 없네요. 우리 재고에 그 책이 없는 거 같네요.

S   그것 참 이상하네요.

C   맞아요. 교수님 성함을 알려주실 수 있나요? 과목 교과서에 대해서 등록된 정보를 찾기 위해 교수님 성함을 집어넣어 볼게요. 그리고 컴퓨터에 뜨는지 봅시다. 그것이 처리되는지 보도록 해요.

S   Kayne 교수님이요.

C   K, A, N, 그리고 E인거죠?

S   아니에요. 스펠링은 K, A, Y, N, E예요. 컴퓨터 공학과에 계세요.

C   컴퓨터 공학과에서 제공되는 수업인가요?

S   네

C   아, 그러면 문제가 뭔지 알겠네요. 길 건너에 있는 컴퓨터 관련 서점에서 컴퓨터 공학과 관련된 책을 팔아요.

S   정말요? 길 건너에요? 왜 제가 본 적이 없죠. 근처에 무슨 간판이라도 세운 게 있나요?

C   잘 모르겠네요.

S   와우, 만약 간판을 세웠더라면, 제가 제 시간이나 당신 시간을 낭비하지 않았을 텐데요.

C   음, 어쨌든, 길 건너편에 있는 컴퓨터 서점을 확인해 보는 것이 좋겠네요. 확신하건대, 거기에 당신 책이 있을 거예요. 만약 그렇지 않다면, 그냥 저에게 다시 오세요. 그러면 다른 장소들에서 그 책을 찾을 수 있도록 도와줄게

different bookstores to see if they have it in their storage. Even if that doesn't work out, I'll place an order online.

S   Oh, yes, you can find anything on the Internet. But then I have to wait for it to be shipped.

C   Hmm... I think the time for shipping is about 2 weeks. I would ask them though, just to be safe.

S   Oh, Ok. Thank you very much, I appreciate it!

요. 다른 서점이 재고가 있는지를 확인해 줄 수 있어요. 만일에 다른 곳에서도 찾을 수 없다면, 인터넷으로 주문을 할 수 있어요.

S   오, 좋아요. 인터넷으로 찾을 수 있다면, 배송을 기다려야만 하는 거죠.

C   음... 제가 알기론 배송 기간이 약 2주일 거예요. 확실하게 하기 위해서 물어보는 게 좋을 거 같네요.

S   정말, 진심으로 감사해요.

1. For what purpose does the student visit the clerk at the bookstore?
   Ⓐ To see which bookstores carry the textbook that he wants to buy
   Ⓑ To request help for finding a textbook for his computer science class
   Ⓒ To ask for directions to the computer bookstore
   Ⓓ To register for additional orders of the book

학생이 서점 직원을 찾아간 목적은 무엇인가?
   Ⓐ 그가 구매하려는 책을 어떤 서점에서 취급하는지 알아보기 위해서
   Ⓑ 그의 컴퓨터 공학 수업을 위한 책을 찾는 데 도움을 요청하기 위해서
   Ⓒ 컴퓨터 서점을 찾는 길을 물어보기 위해서
   Ⓓ 책의 추가 주문을 등록하기 위해서

2. What is the student's initial assumption about why the particular textbook is missing at the bookstore?
   Ⓐ The course that uses the textbook is not part of the university's academic course.
   Ⓑ The course for the book is an advanced level.
   Ⓒ It is a computer related textbook, which is found in the computer bookstore.
   Ⓓ The course he is taking is only offered to the graduate student.

특정 교재를 서점에서 찾지 못한 이유에 대해 학생의 처음 추측은 무엇인가?
   Ⓐ 그 교재를 사용하는 수업이 대학교에서 진행하는 수업이 아니다.
   Ⓑ 그 교재의 수업이 심화 과정이다.
   Ⓒ 컴퓨터 관련 교재는 컴퓨터 서점에서 발견된다.
   Ⓓ 그가 듣는 수업은 오직 대학원생들에게만 제공된다.

3. Why does the student need to purchase this textbook?
   Ⓐ Because the book is a requirement for a class
   Ⓑ Because there will soon be a mid-term exam on the book
   Ⓒ Because the professor already gave out the task on the material
   Ⓓ Because the book is unavailable due to a shortage

학생은 이 교재를 왜 살 필요가 있는가?
   Ⓐ 이 책이 수업의 필수 교재이기 때문에
   Ⓑ 중간고사가 곧 있을 예정이기 때문에
   Ⓒ 교수가 이미 그 교재에서 과제를 내줬기 때문에
   Ⓓ 책이 부족해서 구할 수 없기 때문에

S Oh, yes, you can find anything on the Internet. But then I have to wait to be shipped.

C Hmm... I think the time for shipping is about 2 weeks. I would ask them though, just to be safe.

S 오, 좋아요. 인터넷으로 찾을 수 있다면, 배송을 기다려야만 하는 거죠.

C 음... 제가 알기론 배송 기간이 약 2주일 거예요. 확실하게 하기 위해서 물어보는 게 좋을 거 같네요.

4. What does the woman mean when she says this: 🎧 "Hmm... I think the time for shipping is about 2 weeks. I would ask them though, just to be safe."

Ⓐ She is unable to assist the man any further.

Ⓑ She is not sure she understands the man's question.

Ⓒ She is somewhat certain the shipping time will be too long.

Ⓓ She is uncertain about the length of the delivery.

그녀가 이 말을 한 이유는 무엇인가: "음... 배송 기간이 약 2주일 거예요. 확실하게 하기 위해서 물어보는 게 좋을 거 같네요."

Ⓐ 그녀는 남자를 돕는 게 더 이상 불가능하다.

Ⓑ 그녀가 남자의 질문을 잘 이해했는지 확신할 수 없다.

Ⓒ 그녀는 배달 시간이 길다고 다소 확신한다.

Ⓓ 그녀는 배달 기간에 대해 잘 모른다.

S It's Professor Kayne.

C K, A, N, and E?

S Kayne 교수님이요.

C K, A, N, 그리고 E인 거죠?

5. What is the clerk's main purpose when she asks: 🎧 "K, A, N, and E?"

Ⓐ To clarify the correct spelling of the name of the professor

Ⓑ To confirm that she is referring to the appropriate professor

Ⓒ To ask for the spelling of the textbook auothor's name

Ⓓ To convey that she has never heard of such a professor

직원이 이 질문을 한 의도는 무엇인가: "K, A, N, 그리고 E인 거죠?"

Ⓐ 교수 이름의 정확한 철자를 확인하기 위해서

Ⓑ 그녀가 정확한 교수를 언급하고 있는지 확인하기 위해서

Ⓒ 책의 저자 이름의 철자를 물어보기 위해서

Ⓓ 그녀가 그 교수의 이름을 결코 들어본 적이 없다는 것을 알리기 위해서

Part 2 Questions 6-11

6. Ⓐ	7. Ⓒ	8. Ⓐ, Ⓑ	9. Ⓑ	10. Ⓓ	11. Ⓑ

[Questions 6-11] Listen to part of a lecture in an environmental science class.

P So... let's continue out talk regarding the temperature regulation of the Earth. If you recall our last lecture, I mentioned that researchers are interested in the rise of global temperature and its future impact. There are several factors that affect the Earth's surface temperature and one of these is clouds in the air. A cloud can influence cooling or heating of the Earth's surface. The Earth's climate system automatically maintains the constant balance of cloud's warming and cooling effects.

There isn't too much of a difference, but the primary cumulative function of clouds is to cool the Earth rather than to warm it. This goes through a climate process that balances solar radiation from the Sun that is absorbed by the Earth's surface and then reflected back into space. This process is called the radiation budget. Alongside this we measure something called albedo, on the other side of the planet, in order to keep track of this radiation budget.

The surface's albedo represents the percentage of sunlight, the solar energy that is reflected by cloud back into the space. For instance, Oceans are low in albedo, as they can reflect only a small amount of sunlight. Most of the solar energy that penetrates into the ocean is simply absorbed in to the water. Similarly, the rainforests are also low in albedo. On the other hand, deserts and snow regions have high albedos. In general, clouds have the highest albedos, meaning that clouds reflect tremendous amount of energy back into space.

P 그럼, 지구의 온도 조절에 관한 강의를 계속합시다. 학생들이 지난 강의 내용을 떠올릴 수 있다면, 연구자들은 지구 온도의 증가와 그것의 미래 영향에 대해 흥미가 있다는 것을 제가 언급했습니다. 지구의 표면 온도에 영향을 주는 여러 가지 요소들이 있고 그중 하나는 공기 중의 구름입니다. 구름은 지구 표면의 냉각과 가열에 영향을 줍니다. 지구의 기후 시스템은 자연적으로 온난화와 냉각화에 끊임없는 균형을 유지해 줍니다.

우리가 실제로 알아차릴 만한 큰 차이는 없습니다만, 구름의 주요 기능은 지구를 따뜻하게 해주는 것보다는 차갑게 해주는 데 있습니다. 이것은 지구 표면에 의해 흡수된 후 다시 우주로 반사되는 태양 방사선의 균형을 맞추는 기후 과정을 통해 거치게 됩니다. 이 과정을 복사수지라고 부릅니다. 우리는 지구의 다른 표면의 복사수지를 기록하기 위해 지구의 다른 위치에서 태양광선 방사선이라고 불리는 것을 측정합니다.

표면의 태양광선 방사선은 구름에 의해 반사되서 우주로 돌아가는 태양에너지의 비율을 나타냅니다. 예를 들어, 바다는 작은 양의 태양만 반사하기 때문에 낮은 태양광선 방사능을 갖습니다. 대부분 바다를 통과하는 태양에너지는 바다로 흡수됩니다. 비슷하게 열대우림도 낮은 태양광선 방사능을 갖습니다. 반면에 사막과 눈 있는 지역은 높은 태양광선 방사능을 갖습니다. 일반적으로 구름이 태양광선 방사능이 가장 높습니다. 즉 우주로 돌려보내는 에너지 양이 어마어마하다는 것을 의미합니다.

Alright, now, what I mean by clouds having a high albedo… I'm talking about the reflection of energy that all the clouds on earth cumulatively exert. However, there are different types of clouds; thus there are differences in reflective properties and albedos. Largely, we can divide clouds into two types. There are high altitude clouds, such as the feathery cirrus clouds. And low altitude clouds, such as the stratocumulus clouds that form over cool ocean waters.

S   Then, which type of clouds would cool the Earth and which type would heat it?

P   Well, high and thin clouds would mostly warm up the Earth while low and thick clouds will cool it. High thin clouds are very easily penetrated by the solar radiation in a similar manner to clear air. They have almost no reflective properties; they just simply let radiation pass down to the surface. Also, these clouds have a tendency to trap the earth's heat and generally contribute to heating of the surface.

S   Oh. OK. Then I guess that's because the low thick clouds are not transparent to radiation.

P   Precisely. They reflect most of the sunlight, so very little solar energy reaches the planet's surface.

S   Then, I guess that's how it contributes to cooling.

P   Yes. As I have explained, the cooling effect is the dominant balance effect. Now, there is another factor that controls different types of clouds forming on the Earth. Changes in water vapor, as well as in time of day or time of year, can have a bearing on cloud formation, but did you know that plants might exert an influence as well? Not all types of plants, mind you, but certain species of algae in the sea seem to present a promising

좋습니다. 그럼, 구름이 높은 태양광선 방사능을 갖는다는 것은 어떤 의미인가요… 제가 말하는 것은 지구에 있는 모든 구름들이 축적해서 내보내는 에너지의 반사를 말합니다. 그러나 다른 형태의 구름마다 다른 반사 특징을 갖고 있고 태양광선 방사능에도 차이가 있습니다. 구름은 크게 두 종류로 나눌 수 있습니다. 솜털 모양의 권운 같은 높은 고도의 구름들이 있습니다. 그리고 층적운 같은 낮은 고도의 구름들은 차가운 바다에서 형성됩니다.

S   그러면, 어떤 종류의 구름이 지구를 냉각시키고 어떤 종류가 지구를 가열시킬까요?

P   낮고 두꺼운 구름은 냉각시키는 반면, 높고 얇은 구름들은 대개 지구를 가열시킵니다. 높고 얇은 구름은 태양 방사능을 쉽게 통과시킵니다. 예를 들어 깨끗한 대기처럼요. 그들은 거의 반사하는 특징을 가지고 있지 않습니다. 표면으로 열을 통과시킵니다. 또한 이런 구름들은 지구의 열을 모으는 경향이 있고, 일반적으로 표면의 열에 영향을 줍니다.

S   아, 그러면 제가 생각하기에 낮고 두꺼운 구름은 복사에 투명하지 않기 때문인 거죠.

P   정확해요. 그들은 대부분의 태양을 반사시키고, 거의 지구 표면으로 통과되지는 없습니다.

S   그러면 이것이 냉각의 원인이 될 수 있겠네요.

P   맞습니다. 제가 설명했듯이, 냉각 기능이 전반적인 균형에 영향을 줍니다. 그러면 지구에서 다른 종류의 구름을 형성하는 데 영향을 주는 또 다른 요소가 있습니다. 수증기의 변화와 시간에 따라 구름 형성이 달라집니다. 그러나 식물 또한 영향을 준다는 사실을 알고 있었나요? 물론, 모든 종류의 식물은 아닙니다. 그러나 바다에 있는 특정 종류의 해조류는 연구를 할 만한 가치가 있지요. 우리는 최근에 남극 바다에서 구름의 두께가

area of research. Anyway, we recently found an increase in cloud coverage in Antarctica's oceans. There was a large increase in number of low thick clouds that reflect large amount of solar energy away into space.

It turned out that the reason for the increase in cloud cover was the increasing number of microscopic marine plants. Well, scientists assume that these microorganisms make a chemical called dimethyl sulfide that interacts with the oxygen in the air, resulting in a climate condition that easily allows the formation of low thick clouds. Researchers are still trying to figure out why these marine algae produce dimethyl sulfide and how the gas enters the Earth's atmosphere, but the precise processes are yet unknown. Nonetheless, we are right in a way that this phenomenon has a broad implication. It might even be correct to say that these organisms are controlling the weather. In this sense, if the microorganisms near Antarctica are really the contributors of this phenomenon, we might actually be able to commercialize this mechanism into a technology to manipulate the process of this Earth's cooling and heating. Such commercialization could bring various advantages, such as stabilization of global temperature and economic profit, but little attention is being given to this field. Perhaps with more research, the potential will be recognized in the future.

증가하는 것을 발견했습니다. 대기 중으로 태양 에너지를 반사해 보내는 두껍고 낮은 구름의 숫자가 크게 증가했습니다.

이 구름의 증가 이유는 작은 바다 미세 식물의 수가 증가했기 때문입니다. 과학자들은 이 미생물들이 공기 중에서 산소와 반응하여 쉽게 낮고 두꺼운 구름을 만들어 내는 기후 조건에 영향을 주는 디멘틸설파이드(황화합물)이라고 부르는 화학물질을 만든다고 생각합니다. 연구자들은 아직까지도 왜 이러한 해류들이 황화합물을 만들어 내는지, 어떻게 이 기체가 지구 대기에 들어오는지에 대해 알아내고 있는 중입니다. 하지만 정확한 과정은 아직까지 알려지지 않았습니다. 그럼에도 불구하고 우리는 이 현상의 넓은 의미에 대해서는 제대로 이해하고 있습니다. 심지어 이 유기체가 날씨를 통제한다는 것도 사실일지 모릅니다. 이런 의미로, 만약 남극 지역에 이 미생물이 이 현상에 대한 실제 기여자라면, 우리는 실제로 이 현상을 지구를 냉각 혹은 가열시키는 과정을 조절하는 기술로 상용화시킬 수 있을 것입니다. 이러한 상용화는 지구 온도의 안정화나 경제적인 이윤 같은 다양한 장점을 가져올 수 있습니다만 이 분야에 대한 관심이 낮습니다. 미래에 그 가능성이 실현되기 위해서는 더 많은 연구가 필요할 듯합니다.

Listening
정답 및 해설

어휘_ albedo 태양광선 반사 radiation budget 복사수지 exert (힘을) 가하다 feathery 솜털 같은 cirrus 권운 stratocumulus 층적운 implication 함축, 암시 commercialize 상업화하다 manipulate 조종하다

6. What is the main topic of the lecture?
   Ⓐ The factors that have an influence on a weather phenomenon
   Ⓑ The functional role of certain microorganisms regarding clouds
   Ⓒ The difference between various functions of the low thick clouds and high thin clouds
   Ⓓ The numerous effects and influences of the solar radiation on Earth

강의의 주제는 무엇인가?
   Ⓐ 기상 현상에 영향을 주는 요소들
   Ⓑ 구름에 관련된 특정 미생물의 기능적 역할
   Ⓒ 낮고 두꺼운 구름들과 높고 얇은 구름들의 다양한 기능의 차이
   Ⓓ 지구의 복사수지의 다양한 효과와 영향들

7. According to the professor, how does the albedo help keep track of the radiation budget of the Earth?
   Ⓐ It shows the ratio at which the surface of the Earth reflects and absorbs solar energy.
   Ⓑ It provides mathematical formula for calculating the numerical value of the radiation budget.
   Ⓒ It represents the percentage of solar energy reflection of a certain type of a surface.
   Ⓓ It is a device that captures the amount of solar energy reflection that a surface exerts.

교수의 말에 따르면, 태양 광선반사는 어떻게 지구의 복사수지를 측정하는 데 도움을 주는가?
   Ⓐ 이것은 지구 표면이 태양에너지를 반사시키고 흡수시키는 비율을 보여준다.
   Ⓑ 이것은 복사수지를 계산할 수 있는 숫자로 나타나는 수학 공식을 제공한다.
   Ⓒ 이것은 특정 표면의 태양에너지의 반사율을 나타낸다.
   Ⓓ 이것은 지구 표면이 가하는 태양에너지의 반사양을 측정하는 도구이다.

8. For which two reasons do the high thin clouds contribute to the Earth's heating? Click on 2 answers.
   Ⓐ They are transparent to sunlight and are easily penetrated.
   Ⓑ They tend to capture the solar energy's heat.
   Ⓒ They produce a chemical called a dimethyl sulfide that increases the climate temperature.
   Ⓓ They block the heat that is exerted by the Earth out into the space.

높고 얇은 구름이 지구의 가열에 기여하게 하는 두 가지 요인은 어떤 것인가? 정답을 두 개 고르시오.
   Ⓐ 그것들은 태양 광선에 투명하며 쉽게 통과된다.
   Ⓑ 그것들은 태양에너지의 열을 쉽게 모은다.
   Ⓒ 그것들은 기후 온도를 높이는 디멘틸설파이드라는 화학 물질을 만들어낸다.
   Ⓓ 그것들은 지구에서 우주로 분출되는 열을 막는다.

9. Which of the following is true about the low thick clouds?
   Ⓐ It blocks most of the heat going out of the Earth and contributes to the cooling effect.
   Ⓑ It reflects the heat that comes into the Earth and contributes to the cooling effect.
   Ⓒ It is not transparent to the sunlight and blocks all the light trying to reach the Earth.
   Ⓓ It causes the formation of the dimethyl sulfide produced by a certain marine plant.

다음 중 어떤 것이 낮고 두꺼운 구름에 대한 옳은 설명인가?
   Ⓐ 이것은 지구에서 빠져나가는 대부분의 열을 막고 냉각효과에 기여한다.
   Ⓑ 이것은 지구로 들어오는 열을 반사시키고 냉각효과에 기여한다.
   Ⓒ 이것은 태양빛에 투명하지 않고 지구에 도달하려고 하는 모든 빛을 차단한다.
   Ⓓ 이것은 특정한 해양 식물에 의해서 생산되는 디멘틸설파이드의 형성을 야기한다.

10. What can be inferred about the marine plants that produce dimethyl sulfide?

ⓐ It is currently being harvested by scientists to control the weather on Earth.

ⓑ It is affecting high thin cloud formation by accelerating low thick cloud formation.

ⓒ It is the primary cause for the formation of low thick clouds around the world.

ⓓ It has the potential for practical scientific application to adjust the radiation budget.

디멘틸설파이드를 생산하는 해양 식물에 관하여 추론할 수 있는 것은?

ⓐ 이것은 최근에 지구의 기후를 조절하기 위해 과학자들에 의해 재배되고 있다.

ⓑ 이것은 낮고 두꺼운 구름 형성을 가속화시키면서 높고 얇은 구름의 형성에 영향을 준다.

ⓒ 이것은 세계적으로 낮고 두꺼운 구름 형성의 주된 요인이다.

ⓓ 이것은 복사수지를 조정하여 과학적 실용 가능성을 가진다.

Listen again to a part of the conversation. Then answer the question.

대화의 일부분을 듣고 질문에 답하시오.

---

but did you know that plants might exert an influence as well? Not all types of plants, mind you, but certain species of algae in the sea seem to present a promising area of research.

그러나 식물 또한 영향을 준다는 사실을 알고 있었나요? 물론, 모든 종류의 식물은 아닙니다. 그러나 바다에 있는 특정 종류의 해조류는 연구할 만한 가치가 있지요.

11. Why does the professor say this: 🎧 "Not all types of plants, mind you,"

ⓐ To correct a common misconception

ⓑ To discourage students from guessing

ⓒ To highlight the potential of marine plants over land plants

ⓓ To encourage students to share their opinion

교수는 왜 다음과 같이 말을 했는가?: "물론, 모든 종류의 식물은 아닙니다."

ⓐ 일반적인 오해를 바로잡기 위해서

ⓑ 학생들의 추측을 잠재우기 위해서

ⓒ 육생 식물을 뛰어넘는 해상 식물의 잠재력을 강조하기 위해서

ⓓ 학생들에게 정보 공유를 이끌어 내기 위해서

12. ©   **13.** Ⓐ   **14.** ©   **15.** Ⓐ, Ⓑ   **16.** ©   **17.** Ⓓ

[Questions 12-17] Listen to part of a lecture in a dance history class.

P(Male) In the last class, we've explored the world of classical ballet, in which the dance movements are based on formal and strict positioning of the entire body parts. Today, I want to discuss the modern dance, which is also known to be the theatrical dance.

Now, when the modern dance was introduced and developed during the late nineteenth and the early twentieth century, the audience started paying very serious attention to this new radical form of art.

S(Female) Well, why is this modern dance considered to be radical?

P Let me explain it analogically. Modern dance is like the modern genres of music and art. Unlike the classical predecessors, modern arts would pursue a freer and a more improvisational themes and characteristics. Modern dance concentrates on the natural movement of the body that is inspired by the mood and the feeling of the music. Modern dancers would try to naturally convey a certain emotion or an inspiration to the audience. On the other hand, as I've explained, classical ballet is organized with a set of formal and strictly structured dance movements.

Now, Isadora Duncan, born in 1878, could be considered as the mother of the modern dances. Isadora Duncan, in fact, briefly started her career as a ballerina during her childhood, but eventually came to develop her own special style, which

P(Male) 지난 시간에 우리는 온몸의 외형과 엄격한 위치 설정을 기본으로 움직이는 춤, 고전 발레의 세계를 탐구했습니다. 오늘 저는 연극적인 춤으로 알려져 있는 현대 무용에 대해 논의하고 싶군요.

자, 19세기 말과 20세기 초반 동안 현대 무용이 발달되고 소개되었을 때, 관객들은 새로운 형태의 급진적인 예술에 많은 관심을 갖기 시작했습니다.

S(Female) 음, 왜 이 현대 무용은 급진적으로 여겨졌나요?

P 이것을 비유적으로 설명해 보겠습니다. 현대 무용은 음악과 예술의 현대적인 장르와 같습니다. 고전적인 이전 것들과는 다르게, 현대 예술은 좀 더 자유롭고 더 즉흥적인 주제나 특징을 추구합니다. 현대 무용은 음악의 느낌과 분위기에 영감을 받은 몸의 자연적인 움직임에 집중을 합니다. 현대 무용가들은 관객들에게 특정 감정이나 영감을 자연적으로 전달하려고 했습니다. 반면에, 제가 설명했듯이, 고전 발레는 형식적이고 엄격한 구조로 이루어진 무용의 움직임으로 이루어져 있습니다.

자, 1878년에 태어난 Isadora Duncan은 현대 무용의 어머니라고 할 수 있습니다. Isadora Duncan은 사실 어린 시절에 발레리나로서 그녀의 경력을 짧게 시작했습니다. 하지만, 결국에는 자유 무용이라고 부르는 자신만의 특별한 스타

she referred to as the free dance. When she was fourteen, she perfected this style and started giving lessons to the children and even performed recitals.

In its early stage, the modern dance was based on the collection of natural and somewhat childish movements. For example, it included running, acting out storylines, skipping, and other types of motions such as movements resembling waves that crash onto the shore, or dances that would symbolize trees moving against the wind. These kinds of moves were derived from internal emotion rather than being created by an already organized set of techniques. In fact, Duncan had her hair down while dancing, whereas, Ballerinas would normally tie their hair tightly in a bun. Also, Duncan chose to wear loose and casual outfits, mostly dancing bare foot. On the other hand, ballerinas wore very short skirts and very tight toe shoes. You see, no audience at the time has ever seen Duncan's style of a performance. Duncan gave a lot of variations to her dance when she would perform in various countries. Every performance was different from the previous performances. She quickly became very popular.

In 1904, Duncan started a modern dance school in Berlin. The next year, she went to Russia to perform. What did Russian critics think of her? Unfortunately, it was not really their cup of tea. Unlike much of the contemporary audience who liked her, the Russian critics, most of whom revered Ballet, were skeptical about Duncan's dance, referring to her art form as a pantomime rather than a dance. You see, her style was radically different from ballet. Julie, do you have a question?

S   Yes, why did not Duncan take up ballet? Well, I thought she started studying it during her child hood.

정답 및 해설

일을 개발하게 되었습니다. 그녀가 14살일 때, 그녀는 그의 스타일을 완성하고 아이들에게 강연을 하고 공연을 하기도 했습니다.

초기 단계에서 현대 무용은 자연적이고 어떻게 보면 유치한 움직임의 모음에 기초했습니다. 예를 들어, 뛰고, 이야기의 흐름에 따라 연기하고, 깡총깡총 뛰고 바람에 저항하는 나무의 모양을 상징적으로 표현하는 춤이나 해안가에 부딪히는 파도를 닮은 움직임을 포함합니다. 이런 종류의 움직임은 이미 자리 잡은 일련의 기술들에 의해 만들어지는 것이 아니라 내부의 감정에서부터 만들어진 것입니다. 발레리나들은 일반적으로 헤어핀 안에 머리를 단단하게 묶는 반면, 사실상, Duncan은 춤을 추는 동안 머리를 밑으로 내립니다. 또 Duncan은 대부분 맨발로 춤을 추면서 헐겁고 캐주얼한 옷을 입는 반면, 발레리나들은 매우 단단한 토슈즈와 짧은 치마를 입습니다. 이해할 수 있듯이, 그 당시 어떤 관객도 Duncan의 공연 양식을 본 적이 없었습니다. Duncan은 다양한 나라에서 공연하는 동안 춤에 많은 다양성을 주었습니다. 매 공연은 서로 달랐습니다. 그녀는 빠르게 유명해졌습니다.

1904년에 Duncan은 베를린에서 현대 무용 학교를 열었고 그다음 해에, 러시아로 가서 공연을 했습니다. 러시아 비평가들은 그녀에 대해 어떻게 생각했을까요? 운이 나쁘게도 러시아의 비평가들은 그런 기호가 아니었습니다. 그녀를 좋아했던 많은 동시대의 관객들과는 다르게 대부분 발레를 숭배했던 러시아 비평가들은 Duncan의 예술을 춤이 아닌 팬터마임이라고 말하면서 그녀의 춤에 회의적이었습니다. 아시다시피 그녀의 스타일은 발레와는 급진적으로 달랐습니다. Julie, 질문 있나요?

S   네, 왜 Duncan은 발레를 계속하지 않았나요? 음, 그녀는 어린 시절에 발레를 배우기 시작하지 않았나요?

P As a child, Duncan did not like ballet's restrictive characteristics. Maybe she thought ballet was not creative. When she was in Russia, Duncan was invited to a ballet performance led by Ana Pavlova, a prominent Russian ballerina of the time. Duncan even attended Pavlova's practice session and Duncan was astounded by what she experienced. To Duncan, the ballet exercise and practices seemed overly painful and even excruciating for the health of the dancers who had to maintain an unnatural position for hours. After this experience, Duncan publically criticized ballet for its unnaturally complicated and painful mechanism. In fact, this criticism sparked the beginning of a rivalry between ballet and modern dance. It took a very long time for the rivalry between the two forms of dance to cool down.

P 어릴 적에, Duncan은 발레의 엄격한 특징을 좋아하지 않았습니다. 아마도 그녀는 발레가 창의적이지 않다고 생각했을지도 몰라요. 그녀가 러시아에 있을 때, Duncan은 그 당시 유명한 러시아의 발레리나인 Ana Pavlova가 이끄는 발레 공연에 초대되었고, Pavlova의 연습에도 참석했습니다. 그녀는 자신이 경험한 것에 경악했습니다. Duncan에게 발레 공연과 연습은 과하게 고통스러워 보였고, 수 시간 동안 일반적이지 않은 자세를 유지해야 하는 댄서의 건강이 위험해 보였습니다. 이 경험 후에 Duncan은 공개적으로 발레는 자연적이지 않는 복잡하고 고통스러운 방법이라고 비판했습니다. 사실상, 이 비판은 현대 무용과 발레 사이의 경쟁에 불을 붙였습니다. 이 두 가지 형태의 무용의 경쟁 관계가 가라앉기까지는 꽤 많은 시간이 걸렸습니다.

어휘_ revere 숭배하다 take up 계속하다 excruciating 매우 고통스러운 prominent 유명한

12. What is the lecture mainly about?
  Ⓐ How classical ballet originated from modern dance and music
  Ⓑ The difference between modern dances and classical ballet
  Ⓒ The characteristics of a certain type of performance
  Ⓓ The general public's reaction to modern dances

강의는 주로 무엇에 관한 것인가?
  Ⓐ 현대 무용과 음악이 어떻게 고전 발레에서 유래했는가
  Ⓑ 현대 무용과 발레의 차이점
  Ⓒ 특정 종류의 공연 특징
  Ⓓ 현대 무용에 대한 일반 대중의 반응

13. According to the professor, what can be inferred about modern dances at their early stage?
  Ⓐ They expressed inner emotions freely.
  Ⓑ They required a high level of improvisation.
  Ⓒ They were closely related to contemporary art.
  Ⓓ They shared similar artistic characteristics with classical ballet.

교수의 말에 따르면, 초창기 현대 무용에 관해 유추되는 것은 무엇인가?
  Ⓐ 그들은 내적 감정을 자유롭게 표현했었다.
  Ⓑ 그들은 높은 수준의 즉흥 표현을 요구했었다.
  Ⓒ 그들은 동시대의 예술과 밀접하게 관련되었다.
  Ⓓ 그들은 고전 발레와 유사한 예술적 특징을 공유했었다.

14. According to the lecture, what was the difference between classical ballet and modern dances?
  Ⓐ Unlike classical ballet, modern dance's expressive gestures were derived from strict techniques.
  Ⓑ Modern dances were greatly praised in France while classical ballet was decried in Russia.
  Ⓒ Modern dancers were more free and loose clothing than the classical ballerinas did.
  Ⓓ Modern dances are physically less tiresome than classical ballet.

강의에 따르면, 고전 발레와 현대 무용의 차이는 무엇이었는가?
  Ⓐ 고전 발레와 다르게, 현대 무용은 엄격한 기술에서 파생된 몸짓을 표현했다.
  Ⓑ 현대 무용은 고전 발레가 프랑스에서 외면받은 것과 다르게 러시아에서 몹시 찬사를 받았다.
  Ⓒ 현대 무용수들은 고전 발레리나보다 자유롭고 헐거운 옷을 입었다.
  Ⓓ 현대 무용은 고전 발레보다 육체적으로 덜 성가시다.

15. Why did Duncan dislike ballet?
  Click on 2 answers.
  Ⓐ The ballet technique seemed too strained and uncreative.
  Ⓑ Duncan viewed ballet as a hard and painful form of art.
  Ⓒ Duncan failed as a ballerina during her childhood.
  Ⓓ She personally disliked Pavlova who was a strong figure in the field of ballet.

Duncan은 왜 발레를 싫어했는가?
  정답을 두 개 고르시오.
  Ⓐ 발레 기술이 너무 부자연스럽고 창의적이지 않게 보였기 때문에
  Ⓑ Duncan은 발레를 어렵고 고통스러운 예술로 여겼기 때문에
  Ⓒ Duncan이 어렸을 적에 발레리나로서 실패했기 때문에
  Ⓓ 그녀가 발레계에서 강력한 인물이었던 Pasvlova를 개인적으로 싫어했었기 때문에

16. **For what purpose does the professor mention Ana Pavlova?**
    - Ⓐ To introduce Duncan's childhood rival when she did ballet
    - Ⓑ To provide an example of a person who advocated the modern dances
    - Ⓒ To describe how the competition between modern dances and classical ballet started
    - Ⓓ To emphasize a leading figure of classical ballet in Russia

교수가 Ana Pasvlova를 언급한 이유는 무엇인가?
- Ⓐ Duncan이 발레를 했던 어린 시절 라이벌을 소개하기 위해서
- Ⓑ 현대 무용을 지지한 사람의 예시를 들기 위해서
- Ⓒ 현대 무용과 고전 발레의 경쟁이 어떻게 시작되었는지 설명하기 위해서
- Ⓓ 러시아에서 고전 발레의 거물임을 강조하기 위해서

Listen again to a part of the conversation. Then answer the question.
강의의 일부분을 다시 듣고 질문에 답하시오:

The next year, she went to Russia to perform.
What did Russian critics think of her?
Unfortunately, it was really not their cup of tea.

그다음 해에, 그녀는 러시아로 가서 공연을 했습니다. 러시아 비평가들은 그녀에 대해 어떻게 생각했을까요? 운이 나쁘게도 러시아의 비평가들은 그런 기호가 아니었습니다.

---

17. **What does the professor mean when he says:**
    🎧 **"Unfortunately, it was really not their cup of tea."**
    - Ⓐ Comparatively speaking, Russian critics tend to be very harsh and critical in their reviews.
    - Ⓑ Russian critics were not fond of a foreigner performing in their own country.
    - Ⓒ Russians critics could not refrain from swooning over Duncan's performance.
    - Ⓓ Russian critics denounced performance that went against their taste.

교수가 다음과 같이 말할 때 무엇을 의미하는가?:
"운이 나쁘게도 러시아의 비평가들은 그런 기호가 아니었습니다."
- Ⓐ 비교해서 이야기하자면, 러시아 비평가들은 비평에 관해 무척 모질고 비판적인 경향이 있다.
- Ⓑ 러시아 비평가들은 외국인이 자국에서 공연하는 것을 달가워하지 않았다.
- Ⓒ 러시아 비평가들은 Duncan의 공연에 황홀함을 느끼는 것을 자제할 수 없었다.
- Ⓓ 러시아 비평가들은 그들의 기호에 반하는 공연을 맹렬히 비난했다.

Question 1 / 6

Test3_Speaking_1.mp3

Question Which of the following activities do you think is most beneficial for a child's growth? Playing sport, talking with elders of the community or traveling. Include specific examples and details to explain your answer.

해석 운동하는 것, 지역 사회의 어른과의 대화, 여행 중 아이의 성장에 가장 도움이 되는 활동은 어떤 것이라고 생각하는가? 구체적인 예시와 설명을 통해 답변을 해보시오.

Sample Note-taking

sports

  1) learn coop + gain exp

    → br persp

  2) comp. → stress

    rel. st

Sample Answer

Test3_Speaking_1_Sample.mp3

As **far** as I'm con**cer**ned, / playing **spo**rts is **mo**st **be**neficial / for a **chil**d's **grow**th. / There are **two** reasons for this. /

The **first rea**son is that / playing **spo**rts with **o**thers / will make it **po**ssible for **chil**dren / to **lear**n about **coop**eration / and gain **val**uable experiences / that they've **ne**ver known before. / This would all**ow** them / to **broa**den their perspectives. /

The **se**cond **rea**son is that / children to**day** live in a com**pe**titive world, / and they **al**ways have **loa**ds of work. / **This** is why / they **of**ten feel **dow**n / and stressed **out**. / **But** they can have a **bri**ef moment of rel**ief** / by par**ti**cipating in **spo**rts activities. /

So it would **help** them for**get** about **wo**rries / and make them feel **be**tter. /

해석 내 생각에는, 운동을 하는 것이 아이의 성장에 가장 도움을 준다. 여기에는 두 가지 이유가 있다.

첫 번째 이유로, 다른 사람들과 함께 운동을 하는 것은 아이들이 협동심을 배우고 이전엔 알지 못했던 소중한 경험을 얻게 해준다. 이것은 그들의 시야를 넓힐 수 있게 해준다.

두 번째 이유로, 요즘 아이들은 경쟁 사회에서 살아간다. 따라서 그들은 늘 많은 일에 시달린다. 이 때문에 그들은 우울하고 늘 지쳐 있다. 하지만 운동 활동에 참여함으로써 잠깐의 휴식을 가질 수 있다.

따라서, 이것은 그들이 걱정거리들을 잊고 기분이 나아지는 데 도움을 줄 것이다.

Question 2 / 6

Test3_Speaking_2.mp3

Question Do you agree or disagree with the following statement? People do not need to memorize historical events or references because they can now readily find such information from the Internet. Explain why. Use specific examples and details to support your answer.

해석 사람들은 요즘 인터넷에서 정보를 쉽게 찾을 수 있기 때문에 역사적인 사건이나 근거(참고)를 외울 필요가 없다는 의견에 동의하는가, 동의하지 않는가? 그 이유를 설명하시오. 구체적인 예시와 설명을 통해 답변을 해보시오.

Sample Note-taking

disagree

stressed out

Sample Answer

Test3_Speaking_2_Sample.mp3

Last week, / um… I was **driving** to work, / and **I** was listening to "**Call** to Show" – a **really** famous radio program in Korea, / featuring a re**now**ned educator, Mr. **Par**ker, / stating that it is **ne**cessary for **peo**ple / to memorize his**tor**ical e**ven**ts or **re**ferences. /

At **first**, I **thought** his statement seemed **fair**. / **However**, on **closer** examination, / I believe people do **not** have to memorize / his**tor**ical e**ven**ts or **re**ferences. **This** is because / people to**day** live / in a com**pe**titive world, / and they **al**ways have **loa**ds of work. /

This is why / they **of**ten feel **down** / and stressed **out**. / **Me**morizing his**tor**ical e**ven**ts / would **on**ly make them **more** stressed **out** / when they can find **su**ch infor**ma**tion **ea**sily / on the **In**ternet **now**. /

지난주에, 음... 나는 운전을 하면서 출근하다가 한국에서 굉장히 유명한 라디오 프로그램인 "컬투쇼"를 듣고 있었다. 거기에서 저명한 교육자인 파커 씨가 사람들은 역사적인 사건들이나 근거들을 암기할 필요가 있다고 했다.

처음에는 그의 의견이 맞다고 생각했다. 그런데 곰곰이 생각해보니, 사람들이 역사적인 사건들이나 근거들을 외울 필요가 없다는 생각이 들었다. 왜냐하면 요즘 사람들은 경쟁 사회에서 살아서, 늘 많은 할 일에 시달리기 때문이다.

이 때문에 사람들은 가끔 마음이 우울해지고 스트레스를 받는다. 이제는 인터넷으로 그런 정보를 쉽게 찾을 수 있기 때문에 역사적인 사건이나 근거를 외우는 것은 그들을 더욱 스트레스받게 할 것이다.

Question 3 / 6

Test3_Speaking_3.mp3

Question The woman expresses her opinion about the announcement on banning posters on the walls. State her opinion and explain the reasons why she feels that way.

해석 여자는 벽에 포스터 부착을 금지하는 공지에 대해 의견을 밝히고 있다. 그녀의 의견과 그렇게 느끼는 이유를 설명하시오.

Sample Reading Note-taking

ban stds fr. putting up posters on the walls

- look messy

- use website 4 club ads & bulletin board 4 events

Sample Listening Note-taking

W: X

R1: look nice

- colorful + cool

- show ↑ charac

ex) fr - nice

R2: inconv. b/c bulletin board too far

- dining hall X go

- news deliver X effectively

Sample Answer

Test3_Speaking_3_Sample.mp3

According to the announcement, / the university decided **to ban stu**dents / from **put**ting up **po**sters / on the **wa**lls. /

The **wo**man thinks / the an**noun**cement is a **bad** idea, / and she gives **two** reasons / for holding her opinion. /

The **fi**rst reason she mentions / is that the **po**sters **ac**tually look **ni**ce. / To **be** spe**cif**ic, / they are **co**lorful and **coo**l. / **She** says that the **po**sters / show a **lot** of **cha**rac**te**ri**s**tics / of the s**cho**ol. / (Even one of her **frien**ds from an**o**ther school / **thou**ght that the **po**sters / look **ni**ce.) /

The **se**cond reason she mentions / is that it will be **incon**ve**n**ient for **stu**dents / since the **bu**lletin board / is too far away. / From the **con**ver**sa**tion, / **she** says that / **mo**st **stu**dents do **not** / go to the **di**ning hall, / so she does **not** think / that the **ne**ws will be de**li**vered **effe**ctively. /

So for **the**se reasons, / she thinks this an**noun**cement / is **not** a **good** idea. /

해석 공지에 따르면, 학교는 학생들이 교내 벽에 포스터 부착하는 것을 금지하기로 결정했다.

여자는 이 공지가 좋은 결정이 아니라고 생각해서 이를 뒷받침 할 두 가지 이유를 말한다.

그녀가 말한 첫 번째 이유는 벽에 붙어 있는 포스터들이 보기에 멋있다는 것이다. 자세히 말하자면, 포스터들은 알록달록하고 멋지다. 그녀는 포스터들이 학교의 다양한 특성들을 보여준다고 말한다. 그녀의 다른 학교의 친구는 심지어 포스터가 보기 좋다고 생각했다고 한다.

그녀가 말한 두 번째 이유는 게시판이 너무 멀어서 학생들이 불편하다는 것이다. 대화에서 그녀가 말하기를 대부분의 학생들이 교내의 식당에는 잘 가지 않기 때문에, 정보를 효과적으로 전달할 것이라고 생각하지 않는다.

따라서, 이러한 이유로 그녀는 이 공지가 좋은 결정이 아니라고 생각한다.

Reading

Banning Posters on School Walls

The school has been making an effort to improve the appearance of the campus by working on the gardens and cleaning out the buildings. However, despite the school's efforts, there does not seem to be much of an improvement due to all kinds of posters on the campus walls. Therefore, the school has decided to ban students from putting up posters on the walls. We will make a separate bulletin board in the dining hall for advertising events on campus. Students who want to advertise their clubs should use the school website. We will be making a separate link on the website for advertising clubs.

학교 벽에 포스터 금지

학교 당국은 정원을 가꾸고 빌딩을 청소함으로써 캠퍼스의 외관을 개선시키기 위해 노력을 해왔다. 하지만 학교의 노력에도 불구하고 캠퍼스 벽에 있는 온갖 포스터들 때문에 그다지 큰 개선이 이뤄지지 않는 것처럼 보인다. 따라서 학교는 학생들이 벽에 포스터를 붙이는 것을 금지시키기로 결정했다. 우리는 식당에 교내 광고 행사를 위한 별도의 게시판을 만들 것이다. 자신들의 클럽을 홍보하고 싶은 학생들은 학교 웹 사이트를 이용하면 된다. 클럽 홍보를 위한 메뉴에 대해 웹 사이트에 별도 링크를 만들 것이다.

Listening Script

Test3_Speaking_3_Listening.mp3

W Hey, Logan.

M Hi. Did you see the announcement about banning posters on walls?

W I did. I was surprised that the school made such a decision.

M I did too.

W I don't understand why the school thinks that the posters make the school look messier. I thought having posters up on walls looked quite nice. It made the school more colorful and cool. With all those posters, the school seemed to have more character.

M I know. Students put in a lot of effort into the posters to make them look really nice.

W I remember seeing a poster for the computer

W 안녕, 로건.

M 안녕. 벽에 포스터 부착을 금지한다는 공지 봤어?

W 응. 나는 학교가 그런 결정을 내렸다는 것에 놀랐어.

M 나도 그랬어.

W 학교에서 왜 포스터들이 학교를 더 지저분하게 만든다고 생각하는지 이해가 안 가. 벽에 포스터 있는 것들이 꽤 근사해 보인다고 생각했거든. 포스터들이 학교를 더 다채롭고 멋있어 보이게 해. 모든 포스터들 때문에 학교는 훨씬 개성 있게 보였어.

M 나도 알아. 학생들은 포스터들을 정말 좋게 만들기 위해 많은 노력을 쏟거든.

W 컴퓨터 디자인 클럽의 정말 멋진 포스

designing club and it was really cool. The effects they used made the poster look really impressive. When one of my friends visited our campus he said the posters looked really nice.

M Oh yeah?

W Also, this change will be really inconvenient for students. Since the bulletin board will be in the dining hall, not many students will be able to see the events that are put up. The dining hall is too far away from everything, you know?

M Most of the students eat at the snack bar or outside and barely go to the dining hall.

W That's exactly what I am saying. The news won't be delivered effectively. We would have to go all the way to the dining hall just to check what kind of events are coming up. That's really inconvenient.

M I hope they think this matter over carefully.

터를 본 기억이 나. 포스터에 사용한 효과는 정말 인상적이었어. 친구들 중 한 명이 캠퍼스를 방문했을 때 포스터들이 정말 멋있다고 했어.

M 그래?

W 게다가, 이 변화 때문에 학생들은 정말 불편할 거야. 게시판이 식당 근처에 있어서 많은 학생들이 게시된 행사를 보지 못할 거야. 식당은 모든 곳에서 너무 멀잖아. 그렇지?

M 대부분의 학생들은 스낵바나 밖에서 먹고 식당에 거의 가지 않아.

W 내 말이 바로 그거야. 이런 소식은 효율적으로 전달되지 않을 거야. 우리는 어떤 이벤트들이 일어나는지 확인하기 위해 식당까지 가야 해. 그건 굉장히 불편해.

M 나는 그들이 이 문제를 주의 깊게 고려했으면 좋겠어.

Question 4 / 6

Test3_Speaking_4.mp3

Question Using points and examples from the lecture, discuss what color defense is.

해석 강의의 요점과 예시를 들어, 보호색이 무엇인지 논의하시오.

Sample Reading Note-taking

color defense
defense mechanism 2 defend themselves fr. pred.
- body col. ≈ 2 background
- bright col. 2 stand out

Sample Listening Note-taking

```
ex) skunks

give off stinky smell

  - stripes : easier 2 rec.

    → rem. app

smell + stripes - assoc.

∴ see stripes - recall nasty smell

  - x bother
```

Sample Answer

Test3_Speaking_4_Sample.mp3

In the **le**cture, / the pro**fe**ssor talks about / **co**lor de**fen**se. / (**Co**lor de**fen**se / is a de**fen**se **me**chanism / that **a**nimals and insects **u**se / to de**fe**nd themselves / from **pre**dators.) /

The pro**fe**ssor gives an e**xa**mple / using **sku**nks / to ex**plai**n the topic. /

He **fir**st says that / **sku**nks have **stri**pes on their **ba**cks, / and the **stri**pes make it **ea**sy / for **o**ther **an**imals / to re**co**gnize them. /

The pro**fe**ssor **then** says that / **an**imals are able to re**mem**ber / the **na**sty smell of **sku**nks / because of the **stri**pes on their backs. / **There**fore, / when**ever the**se animals see **stri**pes a**gain** / they re**call** the **na**sty smell / and do **not bo**ther the skunk. /

This is an e**xa**mple / of **co**lor de**fen**se. /

해석 강의에서 교수는 보호색에 대해서 설명한다. (보호색은 동물과 곤충들이 포식자로부터 자신을 방어하기 위해 사용하는 방어 방법이다.)

교수는 강의 주제와 관련하여 스컹크를 예로 든다.

그는 처음에 스컹크가 등에 줄무늬를 가지고 있으며, 이 줄무늬가 다른 동물들이 스컹크를 알아보기 쉽게 한다고 말한다.

그다음에 교수는 동물들이 스컹크 등의 줄무늬 때문에 끔찍한 냄새를 함께 기억할 수 있다고 말한다. 그러므로, 이 동물들이 줄무늬를 볼 때마다 이 끔찍한 냄새를 떠올리며 스컹크들을 괴롭히지 않는다.

이것이 보호색의 한 예다.

Reading

Color Defense

Color defense is a defense mechanism that animals and insects use to defend themselves from predators. There are different types of color defense. One type is having the animal's body to have a similar color to its background. Another type of color defense is the opposite of the former method. Some animals have bright colors or patterns on their bodies. By standing out from the surrounded environment, they are able to warn predators and remind them that they are capable of attacking or defending themselves. Both of these methods of color defense are very effective in protecting animals from predators.

보호색

보호색은 동물과 곤충들이 포식자로부터 자기 자신을 방어하기 위해 사용하는 방어 기제다. 서로 다른 다양한 보호색들이 있다. 이 중 하나는 동물의 몸이 주변 환경과 비슷한 색을 띤다는 것이다. 보호색의 또 다른 종류는 첫 번째 방법과는 완전히 반대이다. 어떤 동물들은 몸에 밝고 화려한 색이나 무늬를 지닌다. 쉽게 눈에 띄기 때문에 이들은 포식자에게 경고를 주며 공격하거나 스스로 방어할 수 있는 능력을 가진 동물이라는 것을 상기시킨다. 이 두 보호색의 방법 모두 자신들을 포식자로부터 보호할 때에 매우 효과적이다.

Listening Script

Test3_Speaking_4_Listening.mp3

Today, we will be talking about a type of defense mechanism animals use in order to protect themselves from danger. A common method of defense method is color defense. Let's look at skunks as an example. You all know that skunks give off a foul smelling odor to scare away other animals, right? Most people often only think of this bad smell when they think of skunks. Although the nasty smell is a method of defense itself, the white stripes on their backs are also a way for them to protect themselves. The stripes on the back of the skunks make it easier for other animals to recognize them. After these animals experience the terrible smell once, they are able to remember skunk's appearance by the stripes on their backs. The stripes and the bad smell become naturally associated. Therefore, when predators see such animals with white stripes on their backs, they

오늘은 동물들이 위험으로부터 자신을 보호하기 위해 사용하는 방어 기제의 종류에 대해 이야기해 볼 거예요. 방어법의 일반적인 유형은 보호색입니다. 예를 들어 스컹크를 봅시다. 스컹크는 다른 동물들을 쫓아내기 위해서 고약한 냄새를 풍긴다는 것을 다들 알고 있죠? 대부분의 사람들은 스컹크를 떠올릴 때 간혹 이 지독한 냄새만을 생각합니다. 비록 고약한 냄새가 방어 방법이지만, 이들의 등에 있는 하얀색 줄무늬가 이들을 지켜주는 또 다른 방법입니다. 등에 있는 줄무늬로 다른 동물들은 스컹크를 인식하기 쉽습니다. 이 동물들이 스컹크의 지독한 냄새를 맡고 나면, 그들은 스컹크의 등에 있는 줄무늬를 보고 이들을 기억할 수 있습니다. 줄무늬와 지독한 냄새가 자연스럽게 연상되는 것입니다. 그러므로, 포식자들이 등에

recall the nasty smell and refrain from bothering them. This is a clear example of color defense. Now you know that it is also the color of skunks that helps protect their safety, not just the nasty odor they give off in times of danger.

흰 줄무늬가 있는 동물을 보게 되면, 고약한 냄새를 떠올려 이 동물을 괴롭히지 않으려고 합니다. 이것이 바로 보호색을 명확히 설명해 주고 있죠. 이제 스컹크의 안전을 지켜주는 것은 이들이 위기에 처했을 때 뿜어내는 고약한 냄새뿐만이 아니라, 이들의 색이라는 것을 아실 거예요.

Question 5 / 6

Test3_Speaking_5.mp3

Question The woman expresses her feelings about the problem. What is the problem and what are the suggestions that are made? What do you think the woman should do?

해 석 여자는 문제점에 대해서 자신의 의견을 표현한다. 문제점이 무엇이고 제시된 해결책은 무엇인가? 당신은 여자가 어떻게 해야 한다고 생각하는가?

Sample Listening Note-taking

M	W
	P: need to watch Hitchcock
	// cousin come over
S 1. ask friend	.
+ M can do 4 her	
	- cousin too shy
S 2. watch film on ≠ date	
	+ have time
	- X sure if can resched to later

정답 및 해설

127

The **wo**man's problem is / that she **nee**ds to **wa**tch a film / for her **cla**ss, / **but** her **cou**sin is coming **o**ver to **vi**sit. / **So** she does **not know** / what to do. /

The **man** and the woman / come up with **two** possible solu**ti**ons / for the **pro**blem. /

The **fir**st one is / to **ask** a friend / to show her **cou**sin a**rou**nd, / and the **se**cond one is / to **wa**tch the film / on a **diff**erent date. / I think / the **wo**man should choose the **fir**st solution. /

The **fir**st reason is / that her **cou**sin / is a grown **up**. / So if she ex**plai**ns her situation, / I am **sure** her cousin **will** understand. /

The **se**cond reason is / that this is a **good** chance / for her **cou**sin to make **frie**nds. /

These are the reasons / why she should **go** with the **fir**st solution. /

해석 여자의 문제는 수업 때문에 영화를 봐야 하는데 사촌이 놀러 온다는 것이다. 그래서 그녀는 어떻게 해야 할지 모른다.

남자와 여자는 이 문제에 대한 두 가지 가능한 해결책을 생각한다.

첫 번째는 사촌을 구경시켜 달라고 친구에게 부탁하는 것이고, 두 번째는 다른 날 영화를 보는 것이다. 나는 여자가 첫 번째 방법을 선택해야 한다고 생각한다.

첫 번째 이유는 그녀의 사촌은 성인이다. 그래서 그녀가 상황을 설명하면, 사촌이 이해해 줄 거라고 확신한다.

두 번째 이유는 사촌이 새로운 친구를 사귈 좋은 기회이기 때문이다.

이러한 이유들로 여자는 첫 번째 해결책을 선택하는 것이 낫다.

Listening Script

M How is it going, Susan?
W Not so well.

M Why? What is the matter? Are you sick?
W No. It's not anything like that. I have to watch the film Hitchcock today, but my cousin is coming over. I promised to have lunch with her and give her a tour of our campus. I think she wants to apply for a program here.

M 어떻게 지내, 수잔?
W 별로 좋지 않아.

M 왜? 무슨 문제야? 아파?
W 아니. 아니 그런 게 아니라. 오늘 히치콕 영화를 봐야 하는데 사촌이 오늘 오거든. 그녀와 점심을 먹고 학교 구경을 시켜주겠다고 약속했어. 내 생각엔 그녀가 우리 학교에 지원하려는 것 같아.

M Oh. Hmm.. Why don't you ask one of your friends to have lunch with your cousin and give her a tour?

W Well I didn't ask anyone yet.

M If you would like, I could do it for you. I am free in the afternoon, so if you need me…

W Would you do that? That is so kind of you!

M Of course, why not?

W But I don't know. My cousin is really, really shy. I mean incredibly shy. I am not sure if she would feel comfortable having lunch with someone she has never met before.

M I guess that could be a problem then. Do you have to watch that film today? Is it for a class or something?

W It is for a project, and I was going to watch it with my classmates. But I do have some time… The class is not until next week.

M Then you have time!

W True. I should talk to my classmates and try to reschedule the film. I am not sure if they will have time later, though.

M I hope you work it out. Call me if you need me!

M 오. 흠. 네 친구들 중 한 명에게 점심을 네 사촌과 먹고 투어를 해 달라고 부탁하는 건 어때?

W 아직 아무한테도 물어보지 않았어.

M 네가 원한다면 내가 해줄 수 있어. 나는 오후에 한가해서 네가 필요하면….

W 그렇게 해줄 수 있니? 넌 정말 착해!

M 당연하지. 왜 안 되겠어?

W 하지만 잘 모르겠어. 사촌은 정말 무척 부끄럼을 많이 타거든. 정말 많이. 그녀가 한 번도 만나보지 못한 사람과 점심을 먹는 걸 편해할지 모르겠어.

M 그럼 문제가 될 수도 있겠구나. 그 영화를 꼭 오늘 봐야 해? 수업과 관련된 그런 거야?

W 프로젝트 때문이야. 같은 반 친구들과 같이 보려고 했어. 하지만 시간이 있기는 해. 수업은 다음 주에 있거든.

M 그럼 시간이 있구나!

W 맞아. 같은 반 친구들과 얘기해서 영화 보는 일정을 변경해야겠어. 하지만 그들이 나중에 시간이 될지 모르겠어.

M 잘 해결하길 바랄게. 내가 필요하면 전화해!

Speaking

정답 및 해설

Question Using points and examples from the lecture, explain the two benefits of joining a business network.

해 석 강의의 요점과 예시를 들어, 비즈니스 네트워크에 참여하는 것의 두 가지 장점을 설명하시오.

Sample Listening Note-taking

T: join biz network - share expertise

1B: gain access 2 wide skills

　　ex) rest. owner - help w/ finance

　　- contact acct

　　- trust 2 handle fin. Prob.

　　- easier + faster

2B: access 2 other friends

　　- even X acct : assist

　　- gain access 2 2ndary ext. ntwk

Sample Answer
Test3_Speaking_6_Sample.mp3

In the lecture, / the professor talks about / the **two** benefits / of a **bu**siness **ne**twork. /

One benefit is that / people can gain access / to different skills. / **Say,** / there is a restaurant owner / that **nee**ds help / with her finance. / She can con**tact** / an ac**coun**tant / in the **bu**siness **ne**twork. / **This** way, / she can **tru**st that person. / **A**lso, it's a **fa**ster way / to find the **ri**ght person. /

Another benefit is that / people can gain access / to the friends and family / of their **bu**siness network's members. / Going **ba**ck to the first example, / even if the res**tau**rant owner / cannot find an accountant / within the **bu**siness **ne**twork, / someone in the network / can help her / find an accountant. /

These are the **two** benefits / of joining a **bu**siness **ne**twork. /

해석 강의에서, 교수는 비즈니스 네트워크의 두 가지 장점에 관해 이야기한다.

한 가지 장점은 다른 기술로 사람들이 접근할 수 있다는 것이다. 말하자면, 그녀의 재정에 도움이 필요한 식당 주인이 있다. 그녀는 비즈니스 네트워크를 통해 회계사를 연결할 수 있다. 이 방법으로, 그녀는 그 사람을 신뢰할 수 있다. 또한, 이것은 적임자를 찾기에 더 빠른 방법이다.

또 다른 장점은 사람들이 비즈니스 네트워크 일원의 친구나 가족으로 접근할 수 있다는 것이다. 첫 번째 예시와 같이 만약 비즈니스 네트워크에서 식당 주인이 회계사를 찾을 수 없다면, 네트워크 안의 회계사를 찾도록 도울 수 있다.

이러한 것들이 비즈니스 네트워크의 두 가지 장점이다.

Listening Script

Test3_Speaking_6_Listening.mp3

There are a countless number of professions all over the world. These professions require all sorts of different skills. In order to gain more knowledge and expertise, one thing many business people do is to join a business network. This network allows professionals to meet and share their own personal expertise with the other members of the group. Since these people have met each other, before they trust each other, and they trust the network. By joining these networks, professionals receive a lot of benefits. I will talk to you about two of these benefits.

First of all, these networks give professionals access to a wide array of skills that they may not have possessed before. Take, for example, a restaurant owner. If this restaurant owner needs help with her finances, she can easily contact an accountant who is in the same business network as her. The owner already knows this accountant, and she trusts him to handle all of her financial problems. This process is much faster and easier than if the owner had to search for an accountant through advertisements.

이 세상에는 셀 수 없을 만큼의 전문직이 있습니다. 전문직은 여러 가지 다른 능력을 요구합니다. 더 많은 지식과 전문성을 얻기 위해 많은 사업가들은 비즈니스 네트워크에 참여합니다. 이 네트워크는 전문가들이 만나서 다른 구성원들과 자신들의 개인적인 전문 지식을 나눌 수 있게 합니다. 이 사람들은 서로 만난 적이 있기 때문에 네트워크와 서로를 믿습니다. 네트워크에 참여하는 것은 전문가들에게 이익입니다. 저는 두 가지 이익에 대해 이야기할 것입니다.

우선, 이 네트워크를 통해 전문가들이 전에는 없었던 광범위한 능력을 가질 수 있습니다. 식당 주인을 예로 들어 봅시다. 식당 주인이 재정과 관련된 도움이 필요하다면 그녀는 간단히 같은 네트워크에 있는 회계사에게 연락을 하면 됩니다. 식당 주인은 이 회계사를 알기 때문에 그녀의 모든 재정 문제를 믿고 맡길 수 있습니다. 이 과정은 식당 주인이 광고를 통해 회계사를 찾는 것보다 훨씬 빠르고 쉽습니다.

Furthermore, members of a business network have access not only to other members of their network, but also to their friends and family members. For example, even if the restaurant owner's business network doesn't have an accountant, someone else in her network may have a sister who is an accountant that he can recommend. Therefore, another benefit to joining a business network is that professionals gain access to a secondary extended network. The restaurant owner benefits because she received a recommendation through one of the members of her business network.

또한, 비즈니스 네트워크의 구성원은 다른 회원만 아는 것이 아니라 그들의 친구 혹은 가족과도 연결되어 있습니다. 예를 들어 식당 주인의 네트워크에 회계사가 없더라도 누나가 회계사인 구성원이 있을 수 있습니다. 그리고 그 구성원이 자신의 누나를 추천해줄 수 있습니다. 그러므로 네트워크에 참여하는 것의 또 다른 이익은 전문가들이 간접적으로 확장된 네트워크에 접근할 수 있다는 것입니다. 식당 주인은 네트워크에 있는 사람의 추천을 받음으로써 이득을 봅니다.

Task 1

Question Summarize the points made in the lecture, being sure to explain how they cast doubt on specific points made in the reading passage.

해석 이 강의가 독해 지문의 명확한 포인트에 대해 어떻게 이의를 제기하는지 확실하게 설명하면서, 강의 포인트를 요약하시오.

서론

[리딩의 기본입장 및 반박문장] **While the author of the reading passage argues that** taking a lot of folic acid, also known as vitamin B, can be dangerous for three reasons, **the lecturer opposes the reading's assertion with counter views**.

본론 1

[강의 주장 및 부연 설명] **First of all, the speaker argues that** most people need to take folic acid because they are lacking. Moreover, pregnant women and babies need it to grow cells of their bodies. [리딩 지문 반론] **This casts doubt on the reading passage's claim that** intake of a lot of folic acid is more likely to cause diseases like cancer.

본론 2

[강의 주장 및 부연 설명] **Additionally, the lecturer points out that** even though elderly people take in a lot of folic acid, this can cause nothing. Rather, it can be helpful for them to keep their bodies healthier and to prevent illnesses. [리딩 지문 반론] **This refutes the reading passage's assertion that** a large amount of folic acid can be detrimental to old people because it can interfere with taking in other vitamins.

본론 3

[강의 주장 및 부연 설명] **Finally, the professor contends that** intake of folic acid through vitamin pills can be problematic because it makes it difficult for people to absorb folic acid. In fact, eating food including vitamins is much better, and a number of people are not likely to take vitamin capsules regularly. [리딩 지문 반론] **This contradicts the idea presented in the reading passage that** the amount of folic acid people consume can be controlled by taking in vitamin pills rather than eating food. [232 단어]

어휘_ known as ~로서 알려지다 lacking 없는(부족한) regularly 정기(규칙)적으로

서론

읽기 지문의 글쓴이가 세 가지 이유를 들어 비타민 B로도 알려진 엽산을 많이 섭취하는 것은 위험하다고 주장하는 반면, 강의자는 반대 의견을 갖고 읽기 지문에 반대한다.

본론 1

우선, 화자는 대부분의 사람들이 엽산 결핍이기 때문에 엽산을 먹어야 한다고 주장한다. 그녀는 아기들이나 임신한 여자들이 자신들 신체의 세포들을 만드는 데 엽산을 필요로 한다고 덧붙인다. 이는 엽산이 암과 같은 병을 유발할 수 있다는 읽기 지문의 요지에 의심을 불러 일으킨다.

본론 2

게다가, 강의자는 노인들이 많은 엽산을 섭취한다 하더라도, 이는 아무 문제도 일으키지 않을 수 있음을 지적한다. 오히려, 엽산을 많이 먹는 것은 노인들이 그들의 신체를 보다 건강하게 만들고 질병들을 예방하는 데 도움이 될 수 있다. 이는 많은 양의 엽산은 다른 비타민의 흡수를 방해하기 때문에 노인들에게 해롭다는 읽기 지문의 주장을 반박한다.

본론 3

마지막으로, 교수는 비타민제를 통한 엽산 섭취는 사람들이 엽산을 흡수하는 것을 어렵게 만들 수 있기 때문에 문제가 있을 수 있다고 논쟁한다. 그녀는 또한 비타민들을 포함한 음식을 먹는 것이 훨씬 나으며, 많은 사람들이 주기적으로 비타민제를 잘 섭취하지 않을 것이라 언급한다. 이는 읽기 지문에 나타난 사람들이 음식을 먹는 것보다는 비타민제를 섭취하는 것을 통해 그들이 먹는 엽산의 양을 조절할 수 있다는 의견을 반박한다.

Reading Passage	**Folic Acid**

Folic acid – problems	엽산 – 문제들이 있다
Recent studies have shown that too much **folic acid**, also known as vitamin B, can be dangerous to the human body. Although folic acid is normally essential to human health as folic acid is responsible for producing healthy **cells, like with anything else**, too much folic acid can be **hazardous**. High amounts of folic acid can cause many health problems, **especially amongst the elderly**.	최근 연구는 비타민 B로도 알려진 엽산이 너무 많으면 인간의 몸에 해로울 수 있다는 것을 보여주었다. 엽산이 건강한 세포를 만드는 것을 책임지기 때문에 인간의 건강에 일반적으로 필수적임에도 불구하고, 그 어느 것들(다른 것들)처럼 너무 많은 엽산은 위험할 수 있다. 많은 양의 엽산은 특히 노인들 사이에서 건강 문제를 야기할 수 있다.

1. causing diseases e.g.) cancer

First of all, scientists have shown that **high doses of** folic acid can result in many harmful diseases including cancer. Less serious **side effects** include **digestive problems**, **nausea** and **loss of appetite** as the **toxicity** of folic acid is relatively low **in comparison to** other vitamins and minerals. However, if high amounts of folic acid in the body **persist**, problems can worsen quickly.

2. harmful to old people

Also, high amounts of folic acid can be particularly harmful to elders. As older people need a good balance of vitamins and minerals to stay healthy, **an overdose of** folic acid can **magnify** the **symptoms** mentioned above, disrupting the intake of other vitamins. This could further **complicate** problems as they would not be getting other vitamins they need.

3. intake of vitamin pills instead of food

One method to control the amount of intake of folic acid is to use vitamin pills instead of food to get the right amount of folic acid. This is because it is easier to control the amount of folic acid one intakes when using the pills instead of food. Therefore one should depend on vitamins for their daily intake of folic acid.

1. 암과 같은 질병들을 야기함

우선, 과학자들은 높은 함량의 엽산이 암을 포함한 많은 해로운 질병들을 일으킬 수 있다고 보여주었다. 덜 심각한 부작용으로는 소화 문제, 메스꺼움, 식욕부진이 있으며, 이는 다른 종류의 비타민이나 무기질에 비교할 때, 엽산의 독성이 비교적 낮기 때문이다. 그러나, 만약 체내에 많은 양의 엽산이 지속된다면 문제들은 빠르게 악화될 수 있다.

2. 노인들에게 해로움

또한, 많은 양의 엽산은 노인들에게 특히 유해할 수 있다. 노인들은 건강하게 지내기 위해서 비타민과 무기질의 알맞은 균형을 필요로 하기 때문에, 엽산을 과다 복용하는 것은 다른 비타민들의 섭취를 방해하며 위에서 언급한 증상들을 악화시킬 수 있다. 이것은 노인들이 그들이 필요로 하는 다른 비타민들을 얻지 못할 수 있기 때문에 문제들을 더 복잡하게 만들 수 있다.

3. 음식 대신 비타민제로 섭취

엽산의 섭취량을 조절하기 위한 한 가지 방법은 알맞은 양의 엽산을 얻기 위해 음식 대신에 비타민을 사용(섭취)하는 것이다. 이는 왜냐하면 음식 대신 약을 섭취할 때 한 번에 섭취하는 엽산의 양을 조절하는 것이 보다 쉽기 때문이다. 그러므로 사람은 일일 엽산 섭취를 위해 비타민에 의지해야 한다.(비타민제를 섭취해야 한다.)

어휘_ folic acid 엽산 cell 세포 like with anything else 다른 것들처럼 hazardous 위험한 amongst (=among) ~중에 the elderly 노인들 high doses of ~(약)의 고용량 복용 side effect 부작용 digestive problems 소화문제 nausea 메스꺼움 loss of appetite 식욕부진 toxicity 독성 in comparison to ~와 비교해 보면 persist 지속되다 overdose of ~의 과다복용 magnify 확대하다 symptom 증상 along with ~와 함께 intake of ~의 섭취 complicate 복잡하게 만들다

Reading - Flawed

Hello class. Did everyone take your vitamins today? I bet a lot of you are hoping that you didn't take too much vitamin B eh? Haha well, you don't worry too much because although the article mentions many valid concerns on excessive intake of vitamin B, the article is also flawed to a certain degree. Sometimes a lot of folic acid can be a good thing! I'll explain the reasons why.

리딩 – 문제 있음

여러분 안녕하세요. 모두들 오늘 비타민을 드셨나요? 여러분 대다수가 너무 많은 비타민 B를 섭취하지 않았기를 바란다는 것을 장담합니다. 뭐, 너무 걱정하지는 마세요. 왜냐하면 앞선 글이 지나친 비타민 B의 섭취에 대한 많은 타당한 우려들을 언급하고 있기는 하지만, 그 글에는 어느 정도 결함 또한 있습니다. 가끔은 많은 엽산이 좋을 수 있어요! 제가 왜 그런지 이유들을 설명할 겁니다.

1. Most → lack of folic acid
- pregnant mothers, babies need more

This article makes it seem like too many people are getting too much folic acid. In reality, this is not the case. Current statistics show that only about 15% of the population is getting the amount of folic acid they need and everyone else is lacking! Also the article does not mention the fact that pregnant mothers, babies, and young children need extra amounts of folic acid because it is crucial for promoting cell growth.

1. 대부분 → 엽산 부족
– 임신부들, 아기들은 더 필요

읽기 지문에서 많은 사람들이 너무 많은 엽산을 섭취하는 것처럼 보입니다. 실제로, 그렇지는 않습니다. 현재의 통계는 인구의 15% 정도만이 그들에게 필요한 양의 엽산을 섭취하고 있으며, 그 외의 다른 사람들은 엽산이 부족하다는 것을 보여줍니다! 또한 지문은 엽산이 세포 성장을 촉진하는 데 중요하기 때문에, 임신한 산모들이나, 아기들 그리고 어린 아이들이 추가의 엽산을 필요로 한다는 사실을 언급하지 않습니다.

2. not harmful to old people
- keep body young
- prevent diseases

Also, the statement that too much folic acid is especially harmful to the elderly is completely false. In fact, the elderly can consume extremely large amounts of folic acid without being harmed at all! Taking in lots of folic acid helps keep their bodies young and prevent diseases. If anything the elderly people today need to have more folic acid than less.

2. 나이든 사람들에게 해롭지 X
– 몸을 젊게 유지시킴
– 질병들을 예방

게다가, 너무 많은 엽산이 노인들에게 특히 더 유해하다는 진술은 완전히 틀렸습니다.(사실이 아닙니다.) 사실, 노인들은 전혀 피해를 받지 않고도 아주 많은 양의 엽산을 섭취할 수 있습니다! 많은 엽산을 섭취하는 것은 노인들의 신체를 젊게 유지하도록 돕고 질병들을 예방합니다. 오히려 오늘날의 노인들은 엽산을 덜 섭취하기보다는 더 섭취해야 합니다.

3. vitamin pills -> hard to absorb folic acid
- vitamins though food -> better
- many ppl X like taking vitamin pills

3. 비타민 알약 → 엽산 흡수가 어려워짐
– 음식을 통한 비타민 → 더 낫다
– 많은 사람들이 비타민제 섭취를 좋아하지 않음

As for the advice the article gives on taking folic acid through vitamin pills instead of through food, there can be many problems associated with this. You see, taking folic acid through the vitamin capsules makes it harder for the body to absorb the folic acid. Studies show that vitamins absorbed through food have a much more significant effect on the body and is overall healthier. Also, a lot of people don't like to take a dose of a vitamin every day, so they are likely to end up not taking vitamins at all.

읽기 지문은 음식 대신 비타민제(약)를 통해 엽산을 섭취할 것을 조언하고 있지만, 이런 방법에는 관련된 많은 문제점들이 있을 수 있습니다. 여러분도 알다시피 비타민제를 통해 엽산을 섭취하는 것은 신체가 엽산을 흡수하는 것을 더 어렵게 만듭니다. 연구들은 음식을 통해 흡수된 비타민들이 신체에 더 상당한 효과를 내며, 전반적으로 더 건강에 이롭다는 것을 보여줍니다. 또한, 많은 사람들은 매일 비타민을 복용하는 것을 좋아하지 않기 때문에 결국 그들은 전혀 비타민을 먹지 않게 될 수 있습니다.

어휘_ bet ~임이 틀림없다 valid 타당한 to a certain degree 어느 정도 in reality 사실은 statistic 통계 pregnant 임신한 cell growth 세포성장 false 거짓 associated with ~와 관련된 vitamin capsule 비타민 캡슐(알약) take a dose of ~를 복용하다 end up –ing 결국 ~하게 되다

Task 2

Question Do you agree or disagree with the following statement?
Cars (automobiles) have had a greater effect on society than planes have.
Use specific reasons and details to support your opinion.

해석 당신은 다음 글에 동의하는가, 아니면 반대하는가?
자동차들이 비행기들에 비해 더 크게 사회에 영향을 끼쳐왔다.
구체적인 이유와 상세한 설명을 통해 자신의 주장을 설명하시오.

서론

[GS] These days, some people take it for granted that automobiles are a part of our life every day. [Thesis] However, contrary to this idea, I strongly believe that planes have had a greater impact on society than cars have. [Rationale] The rationale behind this is that planes have broadened our outlook and led to the economic development of a country. [GS(General Statement)]: 도입 [Thesis]: 자신의 입장 [Rationale]: 근거, 소개

본론1

[TS] **First of all**, planes have played an important role in broadening our perspectives. [SS] **This is mainly because** compared to driving a car, boarding a plane can expose us to different cultures, thoughts, and lifestyles that we have never known before while flying to other countries. Consequently, we can take a quantum leap in intellectual growth and accept diversity important in an era of globalization. [EG] **From my experience**, when I was in college, I flew to Egypt, far away from my country, Korea. As a result, I learned about a wide variety of unique Egyptian cultures such as Egyptian music, food, and its language. This was because I talked with Egyptian people, tried the traditional meal, and visited the Egyptian national museum. If I had not traveled to Egypt, I would have had a narrow mind and a lack of understanding of the society.

[TS(Topic Sentence)]: 소주제문 [SS(Supporting Sentence)]: 뒷받침 설명 [EG(Example)]: 예시

본론2

[TS] **Moreover**, aircrafts have improved the economic situation of a country. [SS] **An important reason is that**, unlike cars, planes can lead a great number of foreigners to a nation. As a result, many businesses such as restaurants, snack shops, and souvenir stores can have more and more customers especially through tourism. On top of that, a number of jobs related to the stores can be created. [EG] **For example**, the town I lived in suffered from the economic recession. Fortunately, a new airport for numerous airplanes revitalized the local economy by providing numerous employment opportunities ranging from airport securities and ticket sellers of travel attractions in the town, and by bringing more profits to local stores. In addition, several foreign investors bought buildings and started family restaurants and shopping centers because the town became economically promising.

본론 3

[Counter Argument] **Admittedly, those who are against my opinion might assert that** a car requiring only roads to use has been considered one of the most common and convenient means of transportation because people easily use them to commute from their home to their schools or workplaces on a daily basis. [Restatement] **Nevertheless, I firmly believe that** an airplane has been more influential than a car on society. [Summary] **The reason is that** it has enabled us to obtain a wider perspective of the world and to improve the economy. [637 단어]

찬성

❶ 시야가 넓어짐: 비행기로 다른 나라들로 여행을 하며 다양한 문화들을 접할 수 있음

❷ 경제 발달: 비행기 덕분에 많은 해외 관광객들 및 방문자들의 증가 및 관광업 발전

Outline

근거 1	비행기로 여행 – 시야가 넓어짐
설명	비행기로 많은 나라들로 이동 다양한 문화, 생활방식, 관습들에 노출 지구촌화되는 현대사회에 필수적인 다양성을 받아들임
예시	비행기로 이집트로 여행 다양한 이집트의 문화들을 경험(언어, 음식, 음악) 이집트인들과 대화, 박물관 방문, 전통음식을 직접 먹어보면서

근거 2	비행기 – 경제 발달
설명	비행기가 많은 외국인들을 끌어들인다 다양한 사업들의 발전을 이끈다 더 많은 일자리들이 생긴다
예시	경기침체를 겪은 우리 동네 새로운 공항이 지역경제를 활성화시킴 다양한 직업들을 제공 + 수입을 늘려주었다

*사회에 영향력: 자동차 vs 비행기

서론

[도입] 오늘날 몇몇 사람들은 자동차가 우리 일상의 일부라는 것을 당연하게 여긴다. [내주장] 그러나 이러한 생각과는 반대로, 나는 자동차보다는 비행기가 사회에 더 엄청난 영향을 줬었다고 믿는다. [이유(근거) 소개] 이것을 뒷받침하는 이론적 근거는, 비행기는 우리들의 시야를 넓혔고 국가의 경제 발전을 이끌었다는 것이다.

본론 1

[이유 1] 우선 비행기는 우리의 시야를 넓히는 데 중요한 역할을 했다. [뒷받침 설명] 이는 왜냐하면 자동차와 비교할 때, 비행기를 타는 것은 다른 나라로 날아가며 우리가 전에 알지 못했던 다른 문화들, 생각들, 삶의 방식들에 우리를 노출시킬 수 있기 때문이다. 결과적으로 우리는 지식적 성장에 비약적 도약을 할 수 있고 세계화 시대에 중요한 다양성을 받아들인다. [예시] 내 경험에 따르면, 대학생 때, 고국인 한국과 먼 이집

트에 갔다. 그 결과, 나는 이집트 인들과 대화하고, 전통 식사를 해보고, 이집트의 국립박물관을 방문해 보며 이집트 음악, 음식, 언어와 같은 넓은 종류의 독특한 이집트 문화를 배웠다. 만약 내가 이집트를 여행하지 않았더라면 나는 좁은 시야를 가졌을 것이고, 그 사회에 대한 이해도 부족했을 것이다.

본론 2
[이유 2] 게다가, 비행기는 한 나라의 경제상황을 개선해 주었다. [뒷받침 설명] 중요한 이유는, 자동차와는 달리, 비행기는 엄청 많은 사람들을 한 나라로 이끌 수 있기 때문이다. 그 결과, 식당들, 간식가게들, 그리고 기념품점들과 같은 많은 사업들이 특히 관광업을 통해서 더 많은 손님들을 받을 수 있다. 게다가, 그 가게 들과 관련된 일자리들도 창출될 수 있다. [예시] 내가 살았던 지역은 경기침체를 겪었었다. 다행히도 수많은 비행기를 위한 새로운 공항이 공항 안전요원들부터 지역 여행지들의 매표원들까지 다양한 많은 고용기회들을 제공하고 지역 상점들에 많은 이익을 가져다줌으로써 지역경제에 다시 활력을 주었다. 또한, 몇몇 외국 투자자들이 건물들을 샀고, 패밀리 레스토랑들과 쇼핑센터를 시작했다 왜냐하면 그 지역이 경제적으로 유명하게 되었기 때문이다.

본론 3
[상대입장 인정] 인정컨대, 내 의견에 반대하는 사람들은 사용하기 위해 단지 도로만 요구하는 자동차가 가장 흔하고 편리한 교통수단으로 여겨져 왔다고 아마도 주장할지 모른다 왜냐하면 사람들이 쉽게 그것들을 집에서 그들의 학교들과 직장들로 매일 통근(등교)하는 데 사용하기 때문이다. [재주장] 그럼에도 불구하고, 나는 비행기가 좀 더 영향력이 있어 왔다고 강하게 믿는다. [이유 요약] 그 이유는, 그것이 우리가 세계에 대한 더 넓은 시야를 가지는 것과 경제를 개선하는 것을 가능하게 해줬기 때문이다.